★ ★ ★ ★ ★ ★ ★

AMERICAN
TRIVIA

★ ★ ★ ★ ★ ★ ★

ALSO BY RICHARD LEDERER

★ ★ ★ ★ ★
AMERICAN
TRIVIA

★ ★ ★ ★ ★ ★

WHAT WE ALL
SHOULD KNOW
ABOUT U.S.
HISTORY,
CULTURE
& *GEOGRAPHY*

★ ★ ★ ★ ★ ★

RICHARD LEDERER
CAROLINE McCULLAGH

GIBBS SMITH
TO ENRICH AND INSPIRE HUMANKIND

First Edition
16 15 14 13 12   5 4 3 2 1
Text © 2012 Richard Lederer and Caroline McCullagh

Published by
Gibbs Smith
P.O. Box 667
Layton, Utah 84041
1.800.835.4993 orders
www.gibbs-smith.com

Designed by michelvrana.com

Gibbs Smith books are printed on paper produced from sustainable
PEFC-certified forest/controlled wood source. Learn more at www.pefc.
org.
Printed and bound in Hong Kong

Library of Congress Cataloging-in-Publication Data

Lederer, Richard, 1938-
  American trivia : what we all should know about U.S. history, culture &
geography / Richard Lederer, Caroline McCullagh. — 1st ed.
      p. cm.
  ISBN 978-1-4236-2277-2
1. United States—Miscellanea. I. McCullagh, Caroline. II. Title.
E156.L43 2012
973—dc23

                    2011043871

Dedications

To my grandparents, Jacob and Rebecca Perewosky and
William and Nettie Lederer, for coming to America.
—Richard Lederer

To Bill, always to Bill.
—Caroline McCullagh

Acknowledgments

Thanks to David Feldman, Audrea Liszt, Syd Love, and our editor,
Bob Cooper, for their help in making *American Trivia* a better book.

Contents

★ ★ ★ ★

★ ★ ★ ★

Introduction

"WHO IS THIS AMERICAN, THIS NEW MAN?"—*J. Hector St. John de Crèvecoeur*

"AMERICA IS NOT MERELY A NATION BUT A NATION OF NATIONS."—*Lyndon Johnson*

"AMERICA IS SO VAST THAT ALMOST EVERYTHING SAID ABOUT IT IS LIKELY TRUE, AND THE OPPOSITE IS PROBABLY EQUALLY TRUE."—*James T. Farrell*

THE UNITED STATES OF AMERICA, a federal constitutional republic covering 3.79 million square miles, is home to a population of almost 315 million people. Our nation is composed of fifty states; one federal district: Washington, D.C.; three territories: American Samoa, Guam, and the U.S. Virgin Islands; and two commonwealths: Puerto Rico and the Northern Mariana Islands.

What are the ties that bind together a country as far-reaching and diverse as ours? Throughout our history, we've lived through the best of times, and we've also lived through the worst of times; yet the heart of our society continues to beat mightily.

We are not a people made from a single stock. Rather, we are a medley of colors, races, religions, and ethnicities. As Jesse Jackson explains, "Our flag is red, white, and blue, but our nation is a rainbow—red, yellow, brown, black, and white."

You might think our language unites us, but in fact we have no official language; we speak all the languages of the world. Walking down the street in any American city, you may hear Spanish or Chinese or Yiddish or any of the more than three

hundred other tongues spoken in the United States. Many people are in the process of transition from the language of their birth to English, while others strive to preserve the language of their heritage.

Is there such a thing as an American palate? We all know what hamburgers, hot dogs, and french fries are, but do you know what a cat biscuit or a johnnycake is? Have you eaten poi? Gyros? Moose hash? Mountain oysters? Gefilte fish? Some of us would say yes, most of us, no.

How about the arts? Do you like music?—Classical? Country? Blues? Rap? Rock? Jazz? Hip-hop? Folk? There's something for everyone. Do you enjoy movies?—Westerns? Romances? Action films? Foreign films? Art films? Documentaries? Animation? The choices seem endless. The same can be said for our literature, our fine arts, our theater, and our dance.

We all share a nation with many people who may look different from us, speak a

"FOR WE MUST CONSIDER THAT WE SHALL BE AS A CITY UPON A HILL. THE EYES OF ALL PEOPLE ARE UPON US."—*John Winthrop, sermon written during the voyage to Massachusetts (1630)*

native language different from ours, and pray in a way that may be foreign to us. In any category you mention, there are a myriad of possibilities. What, then, holds us together in this vast and varied land of ours?

The one thing all Americans have in common is our history. It doesn't matter if you're a first-generation or twelfth-generation American. You own our history. That's what makes you an American. That's the glue that holds us together as a people.

Most of us learn some of that history in school. Then, like so many other facts that we acquired there, the chronicle of our national adventure fades into the background of our lives. Will and Ariel Durant said it best: "We Americans are the best informed people on earth as to the events of the last twenty-four hours. We are not the best informed as to the events of the past sixty centuries."

We hope that this book will make the history of America live for you—that you'll think more about the people who have gone before us and worked so hard to bequeath us a united, spirited, and enchanting country. We hope that you'll find even more precious our national gifts of life, liberty, and the pursuit of happiness.

RICHARD LEDERER AND
CAROLINE MCCULLAGH
San Diego, California

PART 1
Origins

CHAPTER 1

HOW AMERICA GOT ITS NAME

CHRISTOPHER COLUMBUS (1451–1506) is generally given credit for finding America. In grade school most of us learned this ditty:

In fourteen hundred ninety-two,
Columbus sailed the ocean blue.

And he did. On his first voyage, he sighted the Bahamas and made land on Hispaniola (now Haiti and the Dominican Republic). On three subsequent voyages, he also explored the coast of South America. But Columbus never realized that he had sailed to the New World. He died in 1506, blissfully certain that he had reached Asia.

An Italian, **AMERIGO VESPUCCI** (1454–1512), working in Spain for the Medici family, helped outfit the ships for Columbus's first voyage. He in turn

made three voyages to the New World, but never to North America. When he returned to Spain, he wrote about the wonders he had seen.

His account was widely read, even in the Duchy of Lorraine, where Swiss cartographer **MARTIN WALDSEEMÜLLER** (1470?–1520) was drawing a new map of the world. Waldseemüller decided to

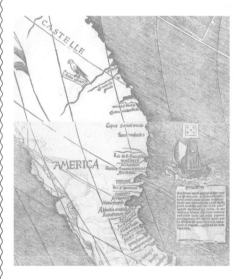

Detail of Waldseemüller's map showing the name "America."

"WHAT THE PEOPLE WANT IS VERY SIMPLE. THEY WANT AN AMERICA AS GOOD AS ITS PROMISE."
—*Barbara Jordan*

write the name *America* across the face of the new continent on his world map. He wished to honor Vespucci because, apparently not having read Columbus's best-selling report of his voyage, he believed Vespucci to be the first man to have set foot in the New World: "Amerigo Vespucci has found another, fourth part, for which I see no reason why anyone could properly disapprove of a name derived from that of Amerigo, the discoverer, a man of sagacious genius." Waldseemüller published a thousand copies of his map in 1507. As far as we know, only one survives, now housed in the Library of Congress.

By the way, *Amerigo* is the Italian form of the Medieval Latin name *Emericus,* which was, in turn, derived from the German *Heimirich—Henry* in English. This may mean that we all actually live in the United States of Henrietta. Could have been worse: Our nation could have been dubbed Vespuccia! ★

CHAPTER 2

IT'S A GRAND OLD FLAG

OUR STAR-SPANGLED BANNER is the most visible symbol of America. Walk through any downtown and you will see the flag flying at the post office, the police station, the fire station, and any number of commercial buildings. Walk through any neighborhood and you may see a flag flying in front of a home. People wear flag pins and flag-themed clothes. Cars sport flag decals. And the flag's stars and stripes, and its colors— red, white, and blue—appear on many products in our stores.

The Second Continental Congress officially adopted the flag on June 14, 1777. The law read "that the flag of the thirteen United States be thirteen stripes, alternate red and white: that the union be thirteen stars white in a blue field, representing a new constellation." The flag served as a maritime flag, used exclusively to identify American ships, until 1834, when the army adopted it as a battle flag. It didn't become a symbol of the nation as a whole until much later.

The first specifications for the American flag, other than that the stars had to be five-pointed, were put forth by President William Howard Taft in 1912. President Dwight Eisenhower established the current flag specifications in Executive Order

"I SEE AMERICA, NOT IN THE SETTING SUN OF A BLACK NIGHT OF DESPAIR AHEAD OF US, I SEE AMERICA IN THE CRIMSON LIGHT OF A RISING SUN FRESH FROM THE BURNING, CREATIVE HAND OF GOD. I SEE GREAT DAYS AHEAD, GREAT DAYS POSSIBLE TO MEN AND WOMEN OF WILL AND VISION."—*Carl Sandburg*

10834 on August 21, 1959, the day Hawaii joined the union as our fiftieth state.

The thirteen stars and stripes of the original flag symbolize the original states. The colors don't officially symbolize anything; but the Great Seal of the United States, adopted on June 20, 1782, uses the same red, white, and blue. The red on the Great Seal signifies hardiness and valor; the white, purity and innocence; and the blue, vigilance, perseverance, and justice.

How the American flag was created is one of the classic stories of the founding of the United States. Some historians give credit to Francis Hopkinson, one of the signers of the Declaration of Independence; but the story of **BETSY ROSS** seems to have captured the imaginations of more Americans. And although there is scant historical proof of the specifics of the story, there is agreement about the course of Betsy's life.

She was born Elizabeth Griscom, the eighth of seventeen children, on January 1, 1752. She was a fourth-generation American, raised as a Quaker and apprenticed to an upholsterer. At twenty-one, she eloped with John Ross, a fellow apprentice. Betsy and John opened an upholstery shop in Philadelphia, where they did general sewing for the home.

William Penn had established Philadelphia ninety-four years previously (in 1682) on the principles of freedom and religious tolerance. When Betsy and John lived there, it was a city of approximately thirty thousand people, including English, Scotch-Irish, Welsh, African American freedmen and slaves, Germans, French Huguenots, Jews, Dutch, and Swedes. Philadelphia was then the second largest English-speaking city in the world after London, and the third most important commercial center in the British Empire, after London and Liverpool. The largest city in the Americas north of Mexico City, it was more populous than New York (which then had approximately five thousand residents) and Boston (approximately seven thousand) combined.

These were times of political ferment. When the Revolutionary War flared up in 1775, John Ross joined a militia. He died in January 1776 when a cache of gunpowder he guarded on the waterfront exploded. After two years of marriage, Betsy was a childless war widow

Two flag designs of the Revolutionary period.

struggling to keep her upholstery business alive.

As the story goes, in May 1776, a committee of the Continental Congress composed of George Washington, Robert Morris, and George Ross, her late husband's uncle, came to Betsy and asked her to make a flag following a sketch that Washington had created. Betsy suggested alterations to the design, in particular changing the six-pointed stars to five-pointed since she could create them with one cut of her scissors. The committee was impressed with Betsy's demonstration, and she began her task and created the first American flag in June 1776. She continued to make American flags for another fifty years as part of her business.

Married and widowed twice more, Betsy Ross bore seven daughters. She retired in 1827, turning the business over to family, and nine years later died at the age of eighty-four. ★

CHAPTER 3

OUR NATION'S BIRTHDAY

THE MOST PROMINENT all-American holiday is the Fourth of July. It's the birthday of our country, and do we ever celebrate! Families gather for parades, picnics, concerts, carnivals, and fireworks.

That national outpouring of jubilation commemorates the signing of the Declaration of Independence. But if you have an image in your mind of a room full of patriots lined up to sign that document on the fourth, think again. That's not how it happened.

The Second Continental Congress, with representatives from the thirteen colonies, was called to order in May 1775. The battles at Lexington and Concord, Massachusetts, had been fought on April 19. Even so, the delegates had little appetite for breaking away from

England. Instead, in July 1775, they sent a petition to King George III asking him to protect them from Parliament, which, in the colonists' eyes, taxed them often and unreasonably. The phrase "no taxation without representation" summed up their complaint.

King George ignored their petition.

On June 11, 1776, a committee was appointed to draft an affirmation of independence. The group included Benjamin Franklin of Pennsylvania, John Adams of Massachusetts, Roger Sherman of Connecticut, Robert Livingston of New York, and Thomas Jefferson of Virginia. Jefferson took on the task of writing the document. All Americans should know the clarion words of the preamble:

We hold these truths to be self-evident, that all men are created equal, that they are endowed by their Creator with certain unalienable Rights, that among these are Life, Liberty, and the pursuit of Happiness.

That statement has been called one of the best-known sentences in the English language and the most potent and consequential words in American history.

After some revisions, the Continental Congress on July 2 voted to accept the declaration of our national sovereignty. As reported in the *Pennsylvania Evening Post,* "This day the Continental Congress

"WHAT IS THE ESSENCE OF AMERICA? FINDING AND MAINTAINING THAT PERFECT, DELICATE BALANCE BETWEEN FREEDOM 'TO' AND FREEDOM 'FROM.'"—*Marilyn vos Savant*

declared the United Colonies Free and Independent States."

On the fourth, John Hancock of Massachusetts, president of the Congress, signed the Declaration of Independence with his prodigious signature in an almost empty chamber. Secretary

Charles Thomson was the only other person who actually signed the Declaration of Independence on July 4, as a witness to Hancock's signature.

On July 8, Hancock read the text to a large and boisterous crowd in Philadelphia. Their joyful response was the first celebration of independence. On July 19, the Continental Congress ordered that the Declaration of Independence be engrossed, or written, on parchment. When that was completed, the document was sent to be signed by the members of the Congress, including John Hancock, on August 2, almost a month after its adoption. Five members signed it later, and two never signed it.

The document marked the formal end of the effort by the American colonies to reconcile with King George. We now considered ourselves to be an independent nation and no longer subjects of the British king.

It was in the Declaration of Independence that the term *The United States of America* was used for the first time. Celebrating the Fourth of July didn't become common until after the War of 1812, and Independence Day wasn't made a federal holiday until 1870. The original parchment copy of the Declaration is housed at the National Archives in Washington, D.C. ★

CHAPTER 4

THE SUPREME LAW OF OUR LAND

THE DOORS AND WINDOWS *of Independence Hall in Philadelphia are closed, protecting the men from the curiosity of those passing by outside. Not a breath of air stirs through the room. Flies buzz in lazy circles. The temperature is eighty-seven and the humidity is high. Sweat beads on faces.*

All around, pairs of men sit at small tables. Some write. The soft scratches of their quill pens disturb neither the concentration of those who sit and think nor those who chat with their neighbors. All stop what they're doing and turn toward the front of the room as the president of the convention stands. George Washington begins to speak. "Gentlemen, let us continue with our discussion. Dr. Franklin, I believe you have the floor."

Independence Hall, Philadelphia.

If only we could have been there to experience that important milestone in the creation of our nation. The Constitutional Convention seems so static when we read about it. In fact, it was alive with passionate debate as the delegates hammered out the details of our future. By mid-June 1787, it became clear that rather than amending the existing Articles of Confederation, forged in 1781 to establish a federal government, the convention would build an entirely new frame of government.

Central government versus states' rights; small state versus large state; slaveholding state versus free state; how to handle public debt, tax collection, trade, and law and order; relationships with foreign governments and with our own Native

Americans—all these controversies had to be addressed. The result was a model of cooperative statesmanship and creative compromise.

Fifty-six men attended the Constitutional Convention, representing Connecticut, Delaware, Georgia, Maryland, Massachusetts, New Hampshire, New Jersey, New York, North Carolina, Pennsylvania, South Carolina, and Virginia. Rhode Island chose not to send delegates.

The Convention began May 25, 1787. On September 17, thirty-nine of the men in attendance signed our Constitution. Washington, as president of the convention, signed first. Then came the representatives of the various states. They understood the importance of what they had wrought, forging a document that begins: "We the people of the United States, in order to form a more perfect Union, establish justice, insure domestic tranquility, provide for the common defense, promote the general welfare, and secure the blessings of liberty to ourselves and our posterity, do ordain

"A THOUSAND YEARS HENCE, PERHAPS IN LESS, AMERICA MAY BE WHAT EUROPE IS NOW: THE NOBLEST WORK OF HUMAN WISDOM, THE GRAND SCENE OF HUMAN GLORY, THE FAIR CAUSE OF FREEDOM."—*Thomas Paine*

and establish this Constitution for the United States of America."

On December 7, 1787, Delaware became the first state to ratify the Constitution; On June 21, 1788, New Hampshire

became the ninth. The Constitution was now the law of the land.

The Constitution of the United States is the oldest written constitution in use in the world. Although we have amended the document twenty-seven times, we the people of the United States have never found it necessary to call for a second Constitutional Convention in all the years since.

Over the years, the engrossed parchment on which the Constitution is inscribed lived in several different places. In 1952, our Constitution was driven in an armored tank under military guard from the Library of Congress to the National Archives, where it remains in a shrine in the rotunda, alongside the Declaration of Independence and the Bill of Rights. ★

CHAPTER 5

A CAPITAL IDEA

IRONICALLY, WASHINGTON was the only president who didn't live in Washington. During George Washington's administration the nation's capital was situated in Philadelphia.

Maryland, in 1788, and Virginia, in 1789, donated a hundred square miles of land to the American government to be used for a capital city. George Washington chose the territory contributed by Maryland, and title to Virginia's land was returned to that state. Before Washington, D.C., was established, the early congresses had met in Philadelphia, Lancaster, and York, Pennsylvania; Princeton and Trenton, New Jersey; Baltimore and Annapolis, Maryland; and New York City.

It was **JOHN ADAMS** who first occupied what was then known as the President's House, at 1600 Pennsylvania Avenue.

John Adams was the first president to list 1600 Pennsylvania Avenue as his home address.

The Adams family moved into their new home on November 1, 1800, while the paint was still drying. Adams occupied the President's House for only four months, having lived most of his term in Philadelphia.

Capital Facts

★ **THEODORE ROOSEVELT** was the first president to call his D.C. home the White House. Previously, the house had been called the President's House or the Executive Mansion. The White

House is the most-visited building in the United States. Graceland, Elvis Presley's former home, is second.

★ In 1814, during the War of 1812, British troops burned the White House. **DOLLEY MADISON** (1768–1849), wife of President James Madison, rescued Gilbert Stuart's famous portrait of George Washington before she fled the city. That most-recognized of all presidential portraits may be the only remaining possession from the original building. The treasure now hangs in the National Portrait Gallery of the Smithsonian Institution.

★ The **WASHINGTON MONUMENT** honors George Washington and, in many people's eyes, symbolizes the city of Washington, D.C. Surrounded by fifty American flags, the monument stands near the center of the National Mall. Towering 555 feet high, this marble obelisk is the tallest stone structure in the world.

The building of the monument began in patriotic fashion on July 4, 1848.

Because of a lack of funds and the onset of the Civil War, construction was halted in 1856 and wasn't resumed for twenty years. The American centennial in 1876 inspired a national passion to complete the obelisk, a goal reached on December 6, 1884, when the final capstone was set. Because marble from one quarry was used from 1848 until 1856 and marble

Gilbert Stuart's famous portrait of George Washington.

"THERE MUST HAVE BEEN SOMETHING SO VERY RIGHT ABOUT AMERICANISM, FOR IN THE DAYS IT WAS PRACTICED, IT BROUGHT US FROM THIRTEEN UNDEVELOPED COLONIES TO THE WORLD'S GREATEST-EVER NATION AND BROUGHT AMERICANS TO NEW HEIGHTS OF LIFE, LIBERTY, AND WELL-BEING."—*J. Kesner Kahn*

from another from 1876 to 1884, a horizontal line about one-third up separates one color from the slightly different color of the top two-thirds.

★ The first **CHERRY TREES** of Washington, D.C., were a gift from the people of Tokyo to the city of Washington. First Lady Helen Herron Taft, along with the Viscountess Chinda, wife of the Japanese ambassador, supervised the planting of the first trees in 1912. Currently more than 3,750 cherry trees of sixteen species adorn the capital.

★ The **SMITHSONIAN INSTITUTION** in Washington, D.C., the largest museum complex in the world, includes museums and galleries, nine research centers, and 160 affiliate museums around the world. Enabled by the bequest of the English chemist James Smithson, it was established in 1846. The Smithsonian comprises sixteen museums in Washington, including the National Air and Space Museum, the National Museum of American History, the National Museum of the American Indian, the National Museum of Natural History, the National Portrait Gallery, and the Smithsonian Institution Building (known as the "Castle"). It also includes the Smithsonian Gardens and the National Zoo in Washington and the Cooper-Hewitt National Design Museum in New York City. With all these museums, it's no wonder that the Smithsonian is sometimes called "the Nation's Attic." ★

CHAPTER 6

NATIONAL SYMBOLS

★ **BENJAMIN FRANKLIN** wanted the wild turkey to be the national bird. In a letter to his daughter after the bald eagle was included in the design of the Great Seal of the United States, he complained that the eagle was "a bird of bad moral character" because it stole food from other birds. The turkey "is in comparison a much more respectable bird ... though a little vain & silly, a bird of Courage." He is even credited with putting forth a case for adopting the rattlesnake as the symbol of the United States in a letter to a magazine in 1775. He wrote that the rattlesnake, unique to America, was a symbol of "wisdom," "vigilance," "magnanimity and true courage."

★ **UNCLE SAM** was first mentioned during the War of 1812. He is thought to have originated in a reference to one Samuel Wilson, who sold beef to the U.S.

J. M. Flagg's iconic Uncle Sam painting was used for this U.S. Army recruiting poster.

Army. J. M. Flagg painted the most famous representation of Uncle Sam for the cover of *Leslie's Weekly* of July 6, 1916. The painting was used to create the famous recruiting poster, prominent in both world wars, that shows Uncle Sam pointing his finger at the viewer and insisting, "I Want You for

Thomas Nast's donkey became the symbol of the Democratic Party.

U.S. Army." A similar patriotic figure, Columbia, was the female personification of the country. She first appeared in 1776, but started fading in popularity by the 1920s. Lady Liberty took her place in the popular imagination.

★ **THOMAS NAST,** perhaps the most famous political cartoonist in our history, was responsible for the popularity of two party animals. During the election of 1828, opponents of President Andrew Jackson labeled him a "jackass" for his populist beliefs. Jackson was entertained by the notion and ended up using it to his advantage on his campaign posters. Nast is credited with making Jackson's donkey the recognized symbol of the Democratic Party through one of his cartoons that appeared in *Harper's Weekly* in 1870. Four years later, also in *Harper's Weekly,* Nast drew a donkey clothed in lion's skin, scaring away all the animals at the zoo. One of those animals, the elephant, was labeled "The Republican Vote." That's all it took for the elephant to become associated with Republicans.

★ In 1752, the colonial province of Pennsylvania paid about $300 for a colossal bell weighing 2,080 pounds, to be cast in England. The first time it was rung, in 1753, it cracked. The great bell was melted down and recast twice in Philadelphia. Its inscription, "Proclaim Liberty throughout all the land unto all the inhabitants thereof," echoes biblical Leviticus 25:10. Traditionally it is thought that the bell was rung on July 8, 1776, to call people together to hear the reading of the Declaration of Independence, but historians doubt that story because the bell steeple was so dilapidated by that time. When British troops captured Philadelphia in September 1777, that bell and all the other bells in Philadelphia were spirited out of town so that the British wouldn't melt them down to make cannons. Once the bell was brought back to the city, it was rung many times to mark important events and anniversaries.

Originally called the Old State House Bell or the Old Independence Bell, it didn't become a national icon until later. The first documented use of the term **"LIBERTY BELL"** appeared in 1839, in a poem published in an abolitionist magazine. The bell cracked again on July 8, 1835, tolling with muffled clapper for the funeral parade of U. S. Chief Justice John Marshall. Now fractured beyond repair, the Liberty Bell is no longer rung, but it is struck on special occasions. On June 6, 1944, when Allied forces landed in France, Philadelphia officials struck the bell, and the tone was broadcast to all parts of the nation. Today the bell hangs in a glass-enclosed structure, Liberty Bell Pavilion, just north of Independence Hall in Philadelphia.

★ The **STATUE OF LIBERTY ENLIGHTENING THE WORLD** was a gift of friendship from the people of France to the people of the United States commemorating the alliance between the two nations during the Revolutionary War. The statue arrived in the United States aboard the French freighter *Isere* as 350 individual pieces packed in 214 crates. Lady Liberty was dedicated on October 28, 1886, designated as a National Monument in 1924, and restored for her centennial on July 4, 1986.

The Statue of Liberty is a universal symbol of freedom and democracy. A bronze plaque inside the base of Liberty displays the Emma Lazarus poem "The New Colossus," written in 1883, with its eternally luminous line: "Give me your tired, your poor, your huddled masses yearning to breathe free":

Not like the brazen giant
of Greek fame,
With conquering limbs astride
from land to land;
Here at our sea-washed,
sunset gates shall stand

A mighty woman with
a torch, whose flame
Is the imprisoned lightning,
and her name
Mother of Exiles. From
her beacon-hand
Glows world-wide welcome;
her mild eyes command

The air-bridged harbor that
*   twin cities frame.*
"Keep, ancient lands, your
*   storied pomp!" cries she*
With silent lips. "Give me
*   your tired, your poor,*
Your huddled masses yearning
*   to breathe free,*
The wretched refuse of your
*   teeming shore.*
Send these, the homeless,
*   tempest-tost to me.*
I lift my lamp beside the golden door!"

Sculptor Frédéric Auguste Bartholdi had modeled Liberty's face on his mother's. The copper skin is ³⁄₃₂ inch thick and is supported by an iron framework designed by Alexandre Gustave Eiffel, the engineer who later designed the Eiffel Tower. In 1876, Liberty's original torch was the first part constructed. In 1984, it was replaced by a new copper torch covered in twenty-four-karat gold leaf, which is lit by floodlights. With a height of 151 feet and a waist 35 feet thick, she may be the most massive woman in America. With her pedestal, the entire Statue of Liberty reaches 305 feet, which made her the tallest structure in the United States when she arrived.

★ From left to right, the images of presidents George Washington, Thomas Jefferson, Theodore Roosevelt, and Abraham Lincoln appear on 5,725-foot-high **MOUNT RUSHMORE,** located in the Black Hills of South Dakota, twenty-three miles southwest of Rapid City. This national monument was created under the direction of sculptor Gutzon Borglum (1867–1941), who worked on the project from 1927 until his death. The heads are about sixty feet high and represent the nation's founding, political philosophy, expansion, conservation, and preservation. The first carving of Jefferson, to Washington's right, was ruined by a flaw in the granite, so it was blasted off the mountain and carved anew on Washington's left. Other problems occurred, and the final carvings were different from what was originally envisioned—representations of the presidents' torsos to the waist. ★

CHAPTER 7

AMERICA SINGING

Fort McHenry and Baltimore Harbor, Maryland.

THE UNITED STATES declared war on Britain on June 18, 1812. Most of us know that conflict as the War of 1812; some historians call it the Second Revolutionary War.

Things were going badly for the American side. In 1814, the British captured Washington, D.C., and burned the White House, the Capitol, the Library of Congress, the Treasury, State, and War Department buildings, as well as other civic buildings. They marched south to Maryland, taking hostages as they went. These hostages, including Dr. William Beanes, were held on British ships outside Baltimore Harbor.

FRANCIS SCOTT KEY, a thirty-five-year-old attorney, was charged with negotiating for his friend Dr. Beanes's freedom. On the orders of President James Madison, he had the use of a ship and help from American prisoner exchange agent Colonel John S. Skinner. His negotiations were successful, but his timing was bad. He was aboard a British ship when

"I DON'T MEASURE AMERICA BY ITS ACHIEVEMENT BUT BY ITS POTENTIAL."
—*Shirley Chisholm*

battle plans were discussed. The captain informed Key that he, Skinner, and Dr. Beanes would not be allowed to go ashore until the battle was over. They would be kept under guard on their own ship for the duration.

Everyone knew that taking Baltimore, an important international port of approximately 50,000 residents, would effectively split the United States in half. British troops on the ground tried but were repulsed. After that, it was the British Navy's turn. Their strategy was to take Fort McHenry at the entrance to Baltimore Harbor. If they did that, Baltimore would be undefended from invasion by sea.

Nineteen British ships rode at anchor in Chesapeake Bay just outside the range of Fort McHenry's guns. They started firing just before dawn on September 13, 1814.

Over the next twenty-five hours, they lobbed between 1,500 and 1,800 shells and rockets into the fort.

Baltimoreans had expected the battle and had been readying themselves for months. New flags for the fort were among the preparations. Major George Armistead, the commanding officer, wanted "a flag so large that the British [would] have no difficulty seeing it from a distance." He got his wish. Mary Pickersgill, a well-known flag maker in Baltimore, made two flags of wool: a smaller storm flag and a larger garrison flag with a hoist of thirty feet and a fly of forty-two. The stripes of the greater flag were two feet wide, and the stars were two feet from point to point. Both flags displayed fifteen stars and fifteen stripes, since Vermont had joined the union in 1791 and Kentucky had separated from Virginia to become a state in 1792.

During the attack on Fort McHenry, four Americans were killed and twenty-four wounded. After the battle, Francis Scott Key waited anxiously on deck for the sun to rise. He'd seen the storm flag flying the previous night as the sun went down. To his joy, he saw that Armistead had raised the huge garrison flag. The battle for control of Baltimore was over, and the Americans had won. As the sun rose on the scene, Key, an amateur poet, expressed his emotions in a poem that he wrote on the back of an envelope. Titled "Defence of Fort M'Henry," those verses were later renamed **"THE STAR-SPANGLED BANNER."**

Most Americans know the first stanza, even though celebrity singers routinely butcher it at sporting events:

Oh! say, can you see,
    by the dawn's early light,
What so proudly we hailed
    at the twilight's last gleaming?
Whose broad stripes and bright stars,
    through the perilous fight,

O'er the ramparts we watched,
    were so gallantly streaming?
And the rocket's red glare,
    the bombs bursting in air,
Gave proof thro' the night
    that our flag was still there.
Oh! say, does that star-spangled
    banner yet wave,
O'er the land of the free
    and the home of the brave?

But you can pick up easy money at almost any gathering of American citizenry by wagering that no one can recite any of the ensuing stanzas:

On the shore, dimly seen
    thro' the mists of the deep,
Where the foe's haughty host
    in dread silence reposes,
What is that which the breeze,
    o'er the towering steep,
As it fitfully blows,
    half conceals, half discloses?
Now it catches the gleam
    of the morning's first beam,
In full glory reflected,
    now shines on the stream.

'Tis the star-spangled banner.
  Oh! long may it wave,
O'er the land of the free
  and the home of the brave!

And where is that band
  who so vauntingly swore,
That the havoc of war
  and the battle's confusion,
A home and a country
  should leave us no more?
Their blood has washed out
  their foul footsteps' pollution.
No refuge could save
  the hireling and slave,
From the terror of flight,
  or the gloom of the grave,
And the star-spangled banner
  in triumph doth wave,
O'er the land of the free
  and the home of the brave.

Oh! Thus be it ever,
  when freemen shall stand,
Between their loved home
  and the war's desolation,
Blest with vict'ry and peace,
  may the Heav'n-rescued land,

Praise the Pow'r that hath made
  and preserved us a nation.
Then conquer we must,
  when our cause it is just,
And this be our motto—
  "In God is our trust."
And the star-spangled banner
  in triumph shall wave,
O'er the land of the free
  and the home of the brave.

Star-Spangled Facts

★ The original copy of "Defence of Fort M'Henry" is displayed at the National Archives.

★ The flag that flew over Fort McHenry and inspired Francis Scott Key is on display at the Smithsonian Institution's National Museum of American History in Washington, D. C. After all the rockets' red glare and bombs bursting in air, that flag has eleven holes in it.

★ "The Star-Spangled Banner" was set to the tune of a British drinking song,

"To Anacreon in Heaven," and was published in 1814 in Baltimore. It became popular immediately.

★ The navy first recognized "The Star-Spangled Banner" for official use in 1889. It was played when the flag was raised.

★ By executive order in 1916, President Woodrow Wilson declared "The Star-Spangled Banner" the national anthem. This meant that the song would be played at all military installations.

★ On March 3, 1931, "The Star-Spangled Banner" was made our official national anthem by a congressional resolution signed by President Herbert Hoover.

★ The motto "In God We Trust" may have been adapted from a line in the fourth stanza of "The Star-Spangled Banner": "And this be our motto—'In God is our Trust.'" It first appeared on a U.S. coin in 1864,

when it was added to the two-cent piece. Over the years, the words were added to more coins, and since 1938, all coins have carried the motto. "In God We Trust" was made the official motto of the United States in 1956, and started appearing on paper currency in 1957, during Dwight D. Eisenhower's presidency.

The obverse of a two-cent piece minted in 1864.

"AMERICANISM IS A QUESTION OF PRINCIPLE, OF IDEALISM, OF CHARACTER; IT IS NOT A MATTER OF BIRTHPLACE OR CREED OR LINE OF DESCENT."—*Theodore Roosevelt*

More Music in the Soundtrack of Our Nation

★ Americans love to sing about their country. Most of us know the tune and at least the opening lyrics to the likes of "When Johnny Comes Marching Home Again," "Dixie," "Battle Hymn of the Republic," "Hail, Columbia," "You're a Grand Old Flag," and "Stars and Stripes Forever."

The first verse of **"YANKEE DOODLE,"** as often sung today, runs:

Yankee Doodle went to town,
Riding on a pony.
He stuck a feather in his hat
And called it macaroni.

The original Yankees were Dutch settlers who had come to the new world, and the term *Yankee* may derive from the Dutch *Jan Kaas,* meaning "Johnny Cheese." *Yankee* migrated from an ethnic insult against the Dutch to New Englanders in general when the song began life as a pre-Revolutionary creation originally sung by British military officers. The intent of "Yankee Doodle" was to mock the ragtag, disorganized New Englanders with whom the British served in the French and Indian War.

Doodle first appeared in the early seventeenth century and derives from the Low German word *dudel,* meaning "fool" or "simpleton." The macaroni wig was in high fashion in the 1770s and became contemporary slang for foppishness. The last two lines of the verse implied that the unsophisticated Yankee bumpkins thought that simply sticking a feather in a cap would make them the height of fashion. The colonists liked the tune of "Yankee Doodle" and adopted it as a robust and proud marching song. What was once a derisive musical ditty became a source of American pride.

★ The lyrics to the soaring song **"AMERICA THE BEAUTIFUL"** were written by **KATHERINE LEE BATES** (1859–1929), a professor of English literature at Wellesley College. While teaching in Colorado in the summer of 1893, she was inspired to write her poem by a view from Pikes Peak. Although Bates never met New Jersey church organist Samuel A. Ward, the music of his hymn "Materna," composed in 1882, was combined with Bates's poem. The two were first published together in 1910.

★ Composer and lyricist Irving Berlin wrote **"GOD BLESS AMERICA"** in 1918 while serving in the U.S. Army at Camp Upton in Yaphank, New York. Berlin created the song for a revue of his titled *Yip Yip Yaphank,* but he set it aside because he believed that the piece was too solemn for his otherwise comedic show. Twenty years later, as the shadow of Adolf Hitler rose to darken the world, Berlin, a first-generation Jewish immigrant, decided to revise his handiwork from a victory song to a peace song. "God Bless America" was introduced and sung by Kate Smith on a 1938 Armistice Day radio broadcast, backed by full orchestra and chorus. It became an instant hit and Smith's signature song. For a while, there was even a movement to make "God Bless America" our national anthem. Rather than raking in profits, Berlin directed that all royalties should go to the Boy Scouts of America and Girl Scouts of the USA. ★

★ ★ ★ ★

PART 2
Hail
to the
Chiefs

★ ★ ★ ★

CHAPTER 8

A PROCESSION OF PRESIDENTS

HISTORIAN HENRY ADAMS, the grandson and great-grandson of presidents, wrote that the president "resembles the commander of a ship at sea. He must have a helm to grasp, a course to steer, a port to seek." The voyages that our American presidents have steered on the ship of state are some of the brightest adventures that any nation has experienced. To begin our exploration of our chief executives, let's review the names of the forty-three men (Grover Cleveland is traditionally counted twice) who have been President of the United States:

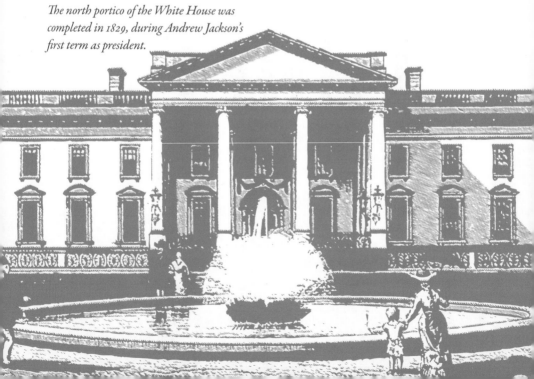

The north portico of the White House was completed in 1829, during Andrew Jackson's first term as president.

1. GEORGE WASHINGTON, 1789–1797
2. JOHN ADAMS JR., 1797–1801
3. THOMAS JEFFERSON, 1801–1809
4. JAMES MADISON JR., 1809–1817
5. JAMES MONROE, 1817–1825
6. JOHN QUINCY ADAMS, 1825–1829
7. ANDREW JACKSON JR., 1829–1837
8. MARTIN VAN BUREN, 1837–1841
9. WILLIAM HENRY HARRISON, 1841
10. JOHN TYLER JR., 1841–1845
11. JAMES KNOX POLK, 1845–1849
12. ZACHARY TAYLOR, 1849–1850
13. MILLARD FILLMORE, 1850–1853
14. FRANKLIN PIERCE, 1853–1857
15. JAMES BUCHANAN JR., 1857–1861
16. ABRAHAM LINCOLN, 1861–1865
17. ANDREW JOHNSON, 1865–1869
18. ULYSSES SIMPSON GRANT, 1869–1877
19. RUTHERFORD BIRCHARD HAYES, 1877–1881
20. JAMES ABRAM GARFIELD, 1881
21. CHESTER ALAN ARTHUR, 1881–1885
22. GROVER CLEVELAND, 1885–1889
23. BENJAMIN HARRISON, 1889–1893
24. GROVER CLEVELAND, 1893–1897
25. WILLIAM McKINLEY JR., 1897–1901
26. THEODORE ROOSEVELT JR., 1901–1909

27. WILLIAM HOWARD TAFT, 1909–1913
28. WOODROW WILSON, 1913–1921
29. WARREN GAMALIEL HARDING, 1921–1923
30. CALVIN COOLIDGE JR., 1923–1929
31. HERBERT CLARK HOOVER, 1929–1933
32. FRANKLIN DELANO ROOSEVELT, 1933–1945
33. HARRY S. TRUMAN, 1945–1953
34. DWIGHT DAVID EISENHOWER, 1953–1961
35. JOHN FITZGERALD KENNEDY, 1961–1963
36. LYNDON BAINES JOHNSON, 1963–1969
37. RICHARD MILHOUS NIXON, 1969–1974
38. GERALD RUDOLPH FORD JR., 1974–1977
39. JAMES EARL CARTER JR., 1977–1981
40. RONALD WILSON REAGAN, 1981–1989
41. GEORGE HERBERT WALKER BUSH, 1989–1993
42. WILLIAM JEFFERSON CLINTON, 1993–2001
43. GEORGE WALKER BUSH, 2001–2009
44. BARACK HUSSEIN OBAMA, 2009–

CHAPTER 9

TEN FASCINATING FACTS ABOUT OUR PRESIDENTS

1. WHAT TWO PRESIDENTS DIED ON THE SAME DAY?

President Thomas Jefferson died on the Fourth of July.

Our second and third presidents—the only two presidential signers of the Declaration of Independence—**JOHN ADAMS** and **THOMAS JEFFERSON**, political rivals, then friends, both died on July 4, 1826, exactly fifty years after the Declaration became official.

As Jefferson lay weak and dying in his home in Monticello on the evening of July 3, he whispered, "Is this the Fourth?" To quiet the former president, his secretary, Nicholas Trist, who was also his grandson-in-law, answered, "Yes." Jefferson fell asleep with a smile. His heart continued to beat until the next day, when bells rang out and fireworks exploded for the Fourth.

At dawn of that same day, Adams was dying in his home in Quincy, Massachusetts. A servant asked the fading Adams, "Do you know what day it is?" "Oh yes," responded the lion in winter. "It is the glorious Fourth of July." He then lapsed into a stupor but awakened in the afternoon and sighed feebly, "Thomas Jefferson survives." He ceased to breathe around sunset, about six hours after Jefferson.

2. WHO WAS THE YOUNGEST MAN EVER TO HAVE SERVED AS PRESIDENT OF THE UNITED STATES?

If your answer is John Fitzgerald Kennedy, you're slightly off the mark.

John F. Kennedy was the youngest man ever to have been elected president.

When he took office, Kennedy was, at the age of forty-three years and seven months, the youngest man ever to have been *elected* president; but **THEODORE ROOSEVELT** became president at forty-two years and ten months, in the wake of the assassination of President William McKinley. When TR's second term was over, he was still only fifty years old, making him the youngest ex-president.

Bill Clinton was our third youngest president (forty-six years and one month), followed, surprisingly, by Ulysses S. Grant (forty-six years and eleven months) and Barack Obama (forty-seven years and one month).

3. NOW THAT YOU KNOW THE IDENTITY OF OUR YOUNGEST PRESIDENT, WHO WAS OUR OLDEST PRESIDENT?

The average age at which America's presidents have taken office is fifty-four. **RONALD REAGAN** became president one month shy of his seventieth birthday, older than any other president, and left office one month shy of his seventy-eighth.

Before Reagan, Dwight Eisenhower had been the only president to reach the age of seventy while in office.

When Ronald Reagan passed away in 2004 at the age of ninety-three years and 120 days, he was our longest-lived president. In 2006, **GERALD FORD** surpassed that record for presidential longevity and lived another month and a half. Amazingly, our third longest-lived president is John Adams, who was born in 1735 and who lived for ninety years and eight months, followed by Herbert Hoover, who lived for ninety years and two months.

President William Howard Taft weighed in at over 300 pounds.

4. WHO WERE OUR TALLEST, HEFTIEST, AND MOST COMPACT PRESIDENTS?

ABRAHAM LINCOLN, at six feet four inches, was our most elevated president, but at six feet and 300 to 340 pounds, **WILLIAM HOWARD TAFT** was our bulkiest president. After he became stuck in the White House bathtub, Taft ordered a new one installed that would accommodate four men of average stature.

Although Taft was our most portly president, he was considered a good dancer and a decent tennis player and golfer.

At five feet four inches and weighing about a hundred pounds (less than a third of Taft), **JAMES MADISON** was our most compact president. The author Washington Irving described Madison as "but a withered little apple-John," but another observer marveled that he had

"THE AMERICAN REVOLUTION WAS A BEGINNING, NOT A CONSUMMATION."—*Woodrow Wilson*

"never seen so much mind in so little matter." In fact, Madison is probably our only president who weighed less than his IQ.

5. HAVE ANY OF OUR PRESIDENTS NOT BEEN BORN CITIZENS OF THE UNITED STATES?

Yes, eight of them. Martin Van Buren, our eighth president, entered the earthly stage on December 5, 1782, making him the first president born after the Declaration of Independence was signed and thus a citizen by birth. Eight presidents were born before 1776 as British subjects—**GEORGE WASHINGTON, JOHN ADAMS, THOMAS JEFFERSON, JAMES MADISON, JAMES MONROE, JOHN QUINCY ADAMS, ANDREW JACKSON,** and, after Van Buren, **WILLIAM HENRY HARRISON.**

6. HAS ANY PRESIDENT RUN AS THE CANDIDATE OF A MAJOR PARTY IN A PRESIDENTIAL ELECTION AND COME OUT THIRD?

In 1912, **PRESIDENT WILLIAM HOWARD TAFT** ran as a Republican for reelection against the Democratic nominee, Woodrow Wilson. Former president Theodore Roosevelt said of his successor,

Woodrow Wilson defeated two major opponents, Theodore Roosevelt and William Howard Taft, in the presidential election of 1912.

"Taft meant well, but he meant well feebly," so Roosevelt also entered the fray, as a candidate for the Bull Moose Party.

Roosevelt and Taft split the Republican vote, and Wilson won handily. Taft placed third with an abysmal 23 percent of the popular vote, the lowest ever for an incumbent president. Unremittingly good-humored, Taft sighed, "I have one consolation. No one candidate was ever elected ex-president by such a large majority."

When William Taft was appointed Chief Justice of the Supreme Court eight years after his presidency, he became the only man ever to have headed both the executive and judicial branches of our government. At their inaugurations, Taft swore in both Calvin Coolidge and Herbert Hoover.

7. HAVE WE EVER HAD A PRESIDENT WHO WAS NEVER ELECTED TO NATIONAL OFFICE?

Richard Nixon resigned from the White House on August 9, 1974, the only president to do so. Spiro Agnew, his vice president, had resigned earlier. As a result of these actions, **GERALD FORD** was, for two years, the only man who served as both vice president (replacing Agnew) and president (replacing Nixon) without having been elected to either office. The

President Gerald Ford was never elected to national office.

"AMERICA HAS NEVER BEEN UNITED BY BLOOD OR BIRTH OR SOIL. WE ARE BOUND BY IDEALS THAT MOVE US BEYOND OUR BACKGROUNDS, LIFT US ABOVE OUR INTERESTS AND TEACH US WHAT IT MEANS TO BE CITIZENS."—*George W. Bush*

only elected office Ford ever held was a western Michigan congressional seat. Ford's vice president, Nelson Rockefeller, who had previously served as governor of New York, was also never elected to national office.

8. HAS ANY PRESIDENT BEEN AN ONLY CHILD?

No American president has remained an only child. All have had at least one full sibling, except for Franklin D. Roosevelt, Gerald Ford, Bill Clinton, and Barack Obama, who have or had half siblings. Twenty-four of our presidents have been first-born males, while six have been the youngest child in their family.

9. HAS ANY PRESIDENT NEVER BEEN MARRIED?

JAMES BUCHANAN was known as the Bachelor President. During his term of office (1857–1861), his niece, Harriet Lane, played the role of First Lady. In 1819, Buchanan had been engaged to Anne Coleman, daughter of the richest man in

James Buchanan was known as the Bachelor President.

Pennsylvania. Through a misunderstanding their engagement was broken off. When Anne died mysteriously a short time later, Buchanan vowed he would never marry. Grover Cleveland also entered the White House as a bachelor but married while he was president.

10. WHAT IS "TECUMSEH'S CURSE"?

William McKinley was the third president to be assassinated in office.

Seven presidents elected in years that end with a zero (intervals of twenty years) died in office—**WILLIAM HENRY HARRISON** (elected in 1840), **ABRAHAM LINCOLN** (1860), **JAMES A. GARFIELD** (1880), **WILLIAM MCKINLEY** (1900), **WARREN G. HARDING** (1920), **FRANKLIN D. ROOSEVELT** (1940), and **JOHN F. KENNEDY** (1960).

First noted in a *Ripley's Believe It or Not* book published in 1931, this string of untimely presidential deaths is variously known as the Curse of Tippecanoe, the Zero-Year Curse, the Twenty-Year Curse, and Tecumseh's Curse. Tecumseh was the Shawnee chief defeated by William Henry Harrison at the Battle of Tippecanoe, Indiana Territory, in 1811.

RONALD REAGAN, elected in 1980 and shot by John Hinckley Jr., almost continued the deadly sequence, but he survived and broke the "curse." Despite being our oldest chief executive, Reagan was the only sitting president to survive a bullet wound. ★

CHAPTER 10
THE PRESIDENTIAL ORIGIN OF *OK*

WHAT MAY BE the most useful expression of universal communication ever devised, *OK* is recognizable and pronounceable in almost every language on earth.

The explanations for the origin of *OK* have been as imaginative as they have been various. But the late language maven Allen Walker Read proved that *OK* did not derive from *okeh,* an affirmative reply in Choctaw; nor from the name of Chief Old Keokuk; nor from a fellow named Orrin Kendall, who manufactured a tasty brand of army biscuit for Union soldiers in the Civil War and stamped them *OK;* nor from the Haitian port Aux Cayes, which produced superior rum; nor from "open key," a telegraph term; nor from the Greek *ola kalla,* meaning "all good."

Rather, as Professor Read pointed out, the truth is more political than any of these theories. He tracked down the first known published appearance of *OK* with its current meaning in the *Boston Morning Post* on March 23, 1839: "The 'Chairman of the Committee on Charity Lecture Balls' is one of the deputation, and perhaps if he should return to Boston, via Providence, he of the Journal, and his train-band, would have

Chief Old Keokuk was not *the inspiration for the expression* OK.

the 'contribution box,' et ceteras, o.k.—all correct—and cause the corks to fly, like sparks, upward."

Allen Walker Read demonstrated that *OK* started life as an obscure joke and through a twist of fate went to the top of the charts on the American hit parade of words. In the 1830s, in New England, there was a craze for initialisms, in the manner of *LOL, OMG, aka,* and *TGIF,* so popular today. The fad went so far as to generate letter combinations of intentionally comic misspellings: *KG* for "know go," *KY* for "know yuse," *NSMJ* for "'nough said 'mong jentlemen," and *OR* for "oll rong." *OK* for "oll korrect" naturally followed.

Of all those loopy initialisms and jocular misspellings, *OK* alone survived. That's because of a presidential nickname that consolidated the letters in the national memory. Martin Van Buren, elected our eighth president in 1836, was born in Kinderhook, New York, and early in his political career was dubbed "Old Kinderhook." Echoing the "oll korrect" initialism, *OK* became the rallying cry of the Old Kinderhook Club, a Democratic organization supporting Van Buren during the 1840 campaign. Thus the accident of Van Buren's birthplace rescued *OK* from the dustbin of history.

The coinage did Van Buren no good, and he was defeated in his bid for reelection. But *OK* has become what H. L. Mencken identified as "the most shining and successful Americanism ever invented." ★

President Martin Van Buren adopted OK *for his 1840 campaign, popularizing the term.*

CHAPTER 11

ABE LINCOLN'S HUMOR

THE MOST FAMOUS DEBATES in American history are the seven between Abraham Lincoln and Stephen A. Douglas campaigning in Illinois in 1858 for a Senate seat. On one occasion, Douglas attempted to buffalo Lincoln by making allusions to his lowly start in life. He told a gathering that the first time he met Lincoln it had been across the counter of a general store in which Lincoln was serving. "And an excellent bartender he was too," Douglas concluded.

When the laughter died away, Lincoln got up and quietly riposted, "What Mr. Douglas has said, gentlemen, is true enough: I did keep a general store and sold cotton and candles and cigars and sometimes whiskey, but I particularly remember that Mr. Douglas was one of my best customers. Many a time I stood on one side of the counter and sold whiskey to Mr. Douglas on the other side. But now there's a difference between us: I have left my side of the counter, but he sticks to his as tenaciously as ever!"

Another difference between the two men was that, two years later, Lincoln defeated Douglas and became our sixteenth president. When Lincoln arrived at the lectern to be sworn in, he held a

"THIS NATION WAS FOUNDED BY MANY MEN OF MANY NATIONS AND BACKGROUNDS. IT WAS FOUNDED ON THE PRINCIPLE THAT ALL MEN ARE CREATED EQUAL, AND THAT THE RIGHTS OF EVERY MAN ARE DIMINISHED WHEN THE RIGHTS OF ONE MAN ARE THREATENED."—*John F. Kennedy*

copy of his speech, his hat, and a cane. He laid down the cane, but there was no place for the hat. Douglas quickly came forward and relieved him of it. As he sat down, Douglas observed to one of Mary Lincoln's cousins, "If I can't be president, I can at least hold his hat."

That Lincoln and not Douglas became president is partly because of Lincoln's subtle humor. A contemporary wrote, "When Lincoln tells a joke in a fireside group, his face loses its melancholy mask, his eyes sparkle and his whole countenance lights up." He referred to laughter as "the joyful, beautiful, universal evergreen of life." In fact, he was our first presidential humorist. During the Civil War, London's *Saturday Review* told its readers, "One advantage the Americans have is the possession of a President who is not only the First Magistrate, but the Chief Joker of the Land."

The common people looked at him as one of their own. A guest at a reception told Lincoln that in his home state people said that the welfare of the nation depended on God and Abraham Lincoln. "You are half right," said

Lincoln. When he was running for the Illinois state legislature, an opponent of considerable standing dwelt on the fact that his father had been a senator, his grandfather a general, and his uncle a congressman. Abe then rose to give his family background: "Ladies and gentlemen, I come from a long line of married folks." And he added, "I don't know who my grandfather was. I am much more concerned to know what his grandson will be."

Years later, when he was asked about what it was like to be president, Lincoln offered an analogy: "I'm like the man who was tarred and feathered and ridden out of town on a rail. When they asked him how he felt about it, he said that if it weren't for the honor of

the thing, he would rather have walked."

Lincoln could impale an opponent with a humorously turned phrase or analogy. "He can compress the most words into the smallest idea of any man I ever met," said Lincoln of a political foe. He once called an argument put forth by Stephen Douglas "as thin as the homeopathic soup that is made by boiling the shadow of a pigeon that has been starved to death."

But Lincoln could make fun of himself, too, especially his gangly height and legendary homeliness. To the inevitable question "How tall are you?" Lincoln would reply, "Tall enough to reach the ground."

"OURS IS THE ONLY COUNTRY DELIBERATELY FOUNDED ON A GOOD IDEA."—*John Gunther*

The *New York Herald* described the president thusly: "Lincoln is the leanest, lankiest, most ungainly mass of legs, arms, and hatchet-face ever strung upon a single frame. He has most unwarrantably abused the privilege which all politicians have of being ugly." During one of the Lincoln-Douglas debates, Douglas accused Lincoln of being two-faced. Replied Lincoln calmly, "I leave it to my audience: If I had two faces, would I be wearing this one?" When a grouchy old Democrat said to him, "They say you are a self-made man," Lincoln riposted, "Well, all I've got to say is that it was a damned bad job."

"When I was a boy," said Lincoln in one of the great debates, "I spent considerable time along the Sangamon River. An old steamboat plied on the river, the boiler of which was so small that when they blew

The young Abraham Lincoln was known for his quick wit.

the whistle, there wasn't enough steam to turn the paddle wheel. And when the paddle went around, they couldn't blow the whistle. My friend Stephen Douglas reminds me of that steamboat, for it is evident that when he talks he can't think, and when he thinks he can't talk."

In the last months of 1862, President Lincoln became angered by the inactivity

"A FREE SOCIETY IS ONE WHERE IT IS SAFE TO BE UNPOPULAR."—*Adlai Stevenson*

of General George B. McClellan's Union forces despite their superior numbers. Exasperated by McClellan's refusal to attack Robert E. Lee and his Confederate forces in Richmond, he wrote the general a one-sentence letter: "If you don't want to use the army, I should like to borrow it for a while. Yours respectfully, A. Lincoln." When a man who wanted to get to Richmond asked Lincoln for a presidential pass, Lincoln responded, "I would be very happy to oblige you if my passes were respected; but the fact is, sir, I have within the last two years given passes to 250,000 men to go to Richmond and not one has got there yet."

In an effort to create the impression of competence and activity, General John Pope reported his plans to Lincoln in a dispatch entitled "Headquarters in the Saddle." Sighed Lincoln: "The trouble with Pope is that he has got his headquarters where his hindquarters ought to be."

General Ulysses S. Grant tipped an occasional glass of whiskey.

Lincoln preferred the fighting spirit of Ulysses S. Grant. A temperance committee visited the president and asked him to fire General Grant. Surprised, Lincoln asked why. "He drinks too much," answered the spokesman for the group. "Well," said Lincoln. "I wish

*Future Supreme Court Justice
Oliver Wendell Holmes Jr.*

some of you would tell me the brand of whiskey that Grant drinks. I would like to send a barrel of it to every one of my other generals."

During the Confederate attack on Fort Stevens in July 1864, Abraham Lincoln journeyed to the front to inspect Union defenses. The task of showing him around fell to young Oliver Wendell Holmes Jr., aide to the commanding general and a future Supreme Court justice. When Holmes pointed out the enemy in the distance, Lincoln stood up—all six feet four of him with a stovepipe hat on top—to have a look. A volley of musket fire spat from the enemy trenches. Grabbing the president by the arm, Holmes dragged him under cover and shouted, "Get down, you fool!" When he realized what he had said and to whom, Holmes was sure that disciplinary action would follow. To his immense relief, Lincoln rejoined, "Captain Holmes, I'm glad to see you know how to talk to a civilian."

When the Civil War ended on April 13, 1865, Lincoln gave orders to stop the draft of soldiers. The following day he made his fatal visit to Ford's Theatre to see *Our American Cousin.* At one point in the play the heroine, reclining on a garden seat, calls for a shawl to protect her from the draft. The actor Edward Southern, to whom the request was addressed, replied on this occasion with this impromptu line: "You are mistaken, Miss Mary. The draft has already been stopped by order of the president!" Lincoln joined in the audience's appreciation of this timely quip with what was to be his last laughter. ★

CHAPTER 12

TR AND THE BEAR FACTS

MOTHERS SEWED STUFFED BEARS before President Theodore Roosevelt came along, but no one called them teddy bears. Not until November 1902, when the president went on a bear hunt in Smedes, Mississippi.

Roosevelt was acting as adjudicator for a border dispute between the states of Louisiana and Mississippi. On November 14, during a break in the negotiations, he was invited by southern friends to go bear hunting. Roosevelt felt that he could consolidate his support in the South by appearing there in the relaxed atmosphere of a hunting party, so he accepted the invitation.

During the hunt, Roosevelt's hosts cornered a bear cub, and a guide roped it to a tree for the president to kill. Roosevelt

Clifford Berryman's famous cartoon.

declined to shoot the cub, believing such an act to be beneath his dignity as a hunter and as a man: "If I shot that little fellow I couldn't be able to look my boys in the face again."

That Sunday's *Washington Post* carried a cartoon, drawn by **CLIFFORD BERRYMAN** (1869–1949), of President Theodore Roosevelt. TR stood in hunting gear, rifle in hand and his back turned toward the cowering cub. The caption read, "Drawing the line in Mississippi,"

"THIS COUNTRY WILL NOT BE A GOOD PLACE FOR ANY OF US TO LIVE IN UNLESS WE MAKE IT A GOOD PLACE FOR ALL OF US TO LIVE IN."
—*Theodore Roosevelt*

referring both to the border dispute and to animal ethics.

Now the story switches to the wilds of Brooklyn, New York. There, Russian immigrants Morris and Rose Michtom owned a candy store where they sold handmade stuffed animals. Inspired by Berryman's cartoon, Rose Michtom made a toy bear and displayed it in the shop window. The bear proved wildly popular with the public.

The Michtoms sent President Roosevelt the very bear they had put in their window. They said it was meant for Roosevelt's grandchildren and asked TR for permission to confer linguistic immortality upon him. The president replied, "I don't know what my name may mean to the bear business but you're welcome to use it."

Rose and Morris began turning out stuffed cubs labeled *Teddy's bear,* in honor of our twenty-sixth president. As the demand increased, the family hired extra seamstresses and rented a warehouse. Their operation eventually became the Ideal Toy Corporation.

The bear was a prominent emblem in Roosevelt's successful 1904 election campaign, and *Teddy's bear* was enshrined in dictionaries in 1907. Cartoonist Berryman never sought compensation for the many uses of the cub he had created. He simply smiled and said, "I have made thousands of children happy; that is enough for me." ★

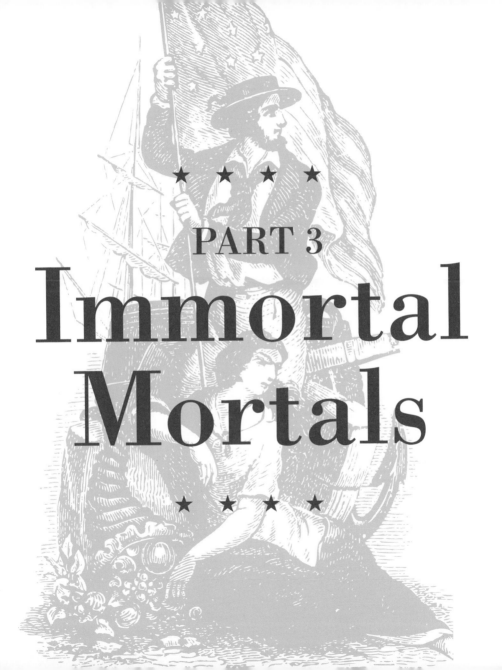

PART 3
Immortal Mortals

CHAPTER 13

THE HOME OF THE BRAVE

A HERO IS A PERSON ADMIRED for his or her courage, nobility, exploits, or achievements and regarded as an ideal or model. Heroes often risk their lives and sometimes die for us. We couldn't do without them.

America seems to be good at making heroes when they're needed. We see them in our daily lives: the police officer, the firefighter, the soldier, and the crusader for a just cause. Sometimes they rise to astonishing heights when circumstances require it. We certainly witnessed extraordinary bravery and sacrifice on 9/11.

Here's a gallery of American heroes who have lit our history with their courage:

★ **JOHN PETER ZENGER** (1697–1746) helped establish freedom of the press in the American colonies. He refused to reveal his sources for a story he published in his newspaper in 1733 criticizing the British governor of New York. To punish him, the British arrested Zenger and tried him in 1735 for criminal libel. Andrew Hamilton, a Philadelphia lawyer, came at the request of Benjamin Franklin to defend Zenger. He argued that publishing the truth could not be libelous. The handpicked judges ordered the jury to find Zenger guilty, but they refused and delivered a verdict of not guilty.

★ **HAYM SALOMON** (1740–1785) was a Polish immigrant who lived and worked in New York City. The British arrested him as a spy in 1776. Pardoned, he was hired to work as an interpreter for the British with their German mercenary troops. Salomon, though, secretly encouraged soldiers to desert and helped prisoners escape. He was arrested again in 1778, tried, and sentenced to death. He escaped to Philadelphia, where he helped finance the Revolution, both by lending large sums of his own money to the fledgling country and by arranging loans from France.

★ **JOHN PAUL JONES** (1747–1792) is often called the Father of the American Navy. He joined the Continental Navy and served as first lieutenant aboard the *Alfred,* the first naval ship bought by the Continental Congress. He later captained the *Bonhomme Richard.* He battled a larger and better-armed squadron of British ships. When the British demanded he surrender, he said "I have not yet begun to fight," and went on to defeat them soundly.

The Father of the American Navy, John Paul Jones.

★ **MARGARET COCHRAN CORBIN**
(1751–1800) became a heroine at the
Battle of Fort Washington in northern
Manhattan on November 16, 1776.
As many wives did, she followed her
husband, John, while he served in the
army, to cook for him, wash his clothes,
and help tend the wounded. John and
another soldier manned one of two
cannons at Fort Washington. When
the two men were killed, Margaret
took their places at the cannon.
Seriously wounded and permanently
disabled, she became the first woman in
America to receive a military pension.

★ **NATHAN HALE** (1755–1776), a Yale-
educated teacher, became a captain in
the Continental Army and a member
of a select group of fighters called
the Rangers. He volunteered to go
through the British lines to gather
intelligence on troop positions in New
York City. At the age of twenty-one,
he was captured and hanged as a spy.
Before he was hanged, he is credited
with saying, "I regret that I have but
one life to give to my country."

*Nathan Hale was only twenty-one years old
when he was hanged by the British.*

"THIS NATION WILL REMAIN THE LAND OF THE FREE ONLY SO LONG AS IT IS THE HOME OF THE BRAVE."—*Elmer Davis*

★ **DAVY CROCKETT** (1786–1836), famous as a hunter, Indian fighter, army scout, and teller of tall tales, described himself as "fresh from the backwoods, half horse, half alligator, a little touched with the snapping turtle." Crockett used his mythic reputation to build a political career, including elected service in the Tennessee legislature and the U.S. House of Representatives. His motto was "Be always sure you're right—then go ahead!" Crockett died at the Alamo fighting for Texas's independence from Mexico. After his passing, he continued to be the subject of songs, books, television programs, and movies.

★ The Lewis and Clark expedition, led by U.S. Army officers **MERIWETHER LEWIS** (1774–1809) and **WILLIAM CLARK** (1770–1838), began near St. Louis on May 14, 1804. The group traveled approximately eight thousand miles, from Missouri to the Pacific Coast and back, exploring the Louisiana Purchase and the Oregon region. A Shoshone Indian, **SACAGAWEA** (1788?–1812), and her French-Canadian husband, Toussaint Charbonneau, accompanied them as interpreters from Fort Mandan in what is now North Dakota. Sacagawea walked thousands of miles

The Lewis and Clark expedition traveled eight thousand miles in two years.

with her infant son, Jean, on her back. The explorers returned to St. Louis in 1806 with maps; specimens; descriptions of plants, animals, and minerals; and information about the peoples of the West, which allowed the United States to establish a better claim of ownership of the Oregon region.

★ **ROBERT E. LEE** (1807–1870) was considered a genius as he rose through the ranks of the U.S. Army. When the Civil War began, President Lincoln offered Lee field command of the army, but he felt duty-bound to stand by his state of Virginia. Although he did not support slavery or secession, he believed that the South, like the original thirteen colonies, was fighting for liberty. He first led the Army of Northern Virginia and then became commander of all Confederate forces. He was beloved by his men and respected by his enemies. On April 9, 1865, Lee surrendered to Ulysses S. Grant at the Appomattox Court House in Virginia and urged Southerners to accept the peace. After the war, Lee became president of Washington College (now Washington and Lee University).

★ **CLARA BARTON** (1821–1912) started her career as a teacher and clerk, but became interested in the health field. During the Civil War, she cared for wounded soldiers on the battlefield. When the war ended, she created a bureau to look for missing men. On a trip to Switzerland, she learned about the Red Cross, based in Zurich. She worked with the organization during the Franco-Prussian War.

Clara Barton helped wounded soldiers during the Civil War.

In 1873, she returned to the United States to facilitate the creation of the American Red Cross. She was president of the organization from 1882 to 1904, when she retired.

★ **ANDREW CARNEGIE** (1835–1919) had to leave school after only three years. His family moved from Scotland to Allegheny, Pennsylvania, when he was fourteen. He started work as a messenger boy for a telegraph company, and, through good luck, he was introduced to Colonel James Anderson, who opened his personal library to young workers on Saturdays. Carnegie educated himself and rose to become one of the richest men in America as the founder of Carnegie Steel Company. In 1901, he sold his company for $480 million. Carnegie believed in philanthropy. Over his remaining years, he gave away more than 90 percent of his fortune. As part of his charitable effort, he founded some three thousand libraries and educated the people to staff them. He also funded construction of seven thousand church organs.

Andrew Carnegie was one of America's greatest philanthropists.

★ **HELEN KELLER** (1880–1968) became blind and deaf at the age of nineteen months because of illness. Wild and unruly, she didn't learn to talk and had no way of communicating. Shortly before Helen's seventh birthday, **ANNE SULLIVAN** (1866–1936), a remarkable teacher, came into her life and remained with her until Anne's death. Anne taught Helen to sign and to read and write in Braille. By the time she was sixteen, she learned to speak. Helen graduated from Radcliffe

"LET EVERY NATION KNOW, WHETHER IT WISHES US WELL OR ILL, THAT WE SHALL PAY ANY PRICE, BEAR ANY BURDEN, MEET ANY HARDSHIP, SUPPORT ANY FRIEND, OPPOSE ANY FOE, TO ASSURE THE SURVIVAL AND SUCCESS OF LIBERTY."—*John F. Kennedy*

College cum laude and became an author, speaker, political activist, recipient of the Presidential Medal of Freedom, and member of the National Institute of Arts and Letters. She traveled and lectured throughout the world, working to improve the lives of the blind and the deaf-blind.

★ **EDDIE RICKENBACKER** (1890–1973) was the leading United States air ace in World War I. Before that, he had been an internationally known race car driver, but in 1917 he joined the army. A pilot must shoot down five enemy aircraft to be counted as an ace. He shot down twenty-two planes and four balloons. In World War II he served again, this time as a civilian inspector of air bases in the United States and overseas. In 1942, he was in a plane that was forced down in the Pacific. Along with six compatriots, Rickenbacker survived twenty-four days in a rubber raft before being rescued.

★ **CHARLES LINDBERGH** (1902–1974) made the first nonstop solo flight from New York to Paris on May 20 and 21, 1927, and won a $25,000 prize offered by a New York

Charles Lindbergh's hop across the Atlantic was the inspiration for the Lindy Hop dance craze.

City hotel owner. Lindbergh, also known as "Lucky Lindy" and "The Lone Eagle," took off in the *Spirit of St. Louis* from Roosevelt Field in Garden City, Long Island. He flew more than 3,500 miles in thirty-three and one-half hours, supplied with only four sandwiches and two gallons of water. Sometimes he flew only ten feet above the water. When he reached Le Bourget Field in Paris, ten thousand Parisians welcomed him. He was an instant hero worldwide. In the United States, he was so popular that a dance craze was called the Lindy Hop.

★ In 1962, **JOHN GLENN** (1921–), a World War II fighter pilot, became the fifth man to travel in space and the first American to orbit the earth. In 1998, after serving twenty-four years in the Senate, Glenn, at age seventy-seven, lifted off for a second space flight thirty-six years after his first mission. His nine-day journey as by far the oldest-ever astronaut was designed to study the effects of space flight on the elderly. ★

CHAPTER 14

THE LAND OF THE FREE

SOME OF OUR ANCESTORS came to the New World to find freedom: freedom of thought, freedom of religion, freedom from the old shackles of caste and class. Others were transported as slaves. Once here, they didn't wait for freedom; they strove to achieve it.

Senator and two-time presidential candidate Adlai Stevenson said half a century ago, "America is much more than a geographical fact. It is a political and moral fact—the first community in which men set out in principle to institutionalize freedom, responsible government, and human equality." Our history is an ongoing chronology of that effort.

★ **SOJOURNER TRUTH** (1797–1883) was born Isabella Baumfree, a slave in Ulster County, New York, and was freed in 1827, when New York outlawed slavery.

Taking the name Sojourner Truth, she became an evangelist and social reformer preaching for abolition and women's rights. She helped many escaped slaves. In 1864, she visited President Abraham Lincoln in the White House. She also received many posthumous honors. A stamp honoring her was issued in 1986; a Mars probe was named after her in 1997; and she was honored with a bust in the U.S. Capitol in 2008.

★ **LEVI** (1798–1877) and **CATHERINE COFFIN** (1803–1881), Quakers in what is now Fountain City, Indiana, welcomed and helped more than three thousand slaves on their way to freedom in northern states and Canada via the Underground Railroad.

★ **ELIZABETH CADY STANTON** (1815–1902) led the early battle for women's suffrage and for the abolition of slavery. She and **LUCRETIA MOTT** (1793–1880) organized the 1848 Seneca Falls Convention, the nation's first public women's rights meeting. In 1865, she broke with the abolitionists, who

Elizabeth Cady Stanton was an early crusader for women's suffrage.

favored allowing voting for African Americans but not for women. In 1869, Stanton and **SUSAN B. ANTHONY** (1820-1906) founded the National Woman Suffrage Association. Stanton served as president of the association and its successor organization, the National American Woman Suffrage Association, for more than thirty years. None of the three women lived to see the 1919 adoption of the Nineteenth Amendment to the Constitution granting women the right to vote.

★ **FREDERICK DOUGLASS** (1818–1895) escaped from his slave master in 1838. Three years later, he spoke eloquently about freedom at a meeting of the Massachusetts Anti-Slavery Society, which immediately hired him to

Frederick Douglass helped recruit African American soldiers for the Union Army.

travel and lecture about being a slave. He protested segregation on trains and in churches. In 1845, Douglass published his first autobiography, *Narrative of the Life of Frederick Douglass, an American Slave.* Fearing capture when the book was released, he fled to England and Ireland, where he earned enough money to return to the United States in 1847 to buy his freedom. He founded several antislavery newspapers, including the *North Star* in Rochester, New York, and continued to speak and work against slavery and discrimination. During the Civil War, Douglass helped recruit African Americans for the Union Army and consulted several times with President Lincoln. After the war, he worked to gain civil rights for former slaves. He also supported the cause of women's suffrage.

★ Born a slave, **HARRIET TUBMAN** (1820?–1913) escaped in 1849 and went to Philadelphia. In 1850, she made the first of nineteen trips south to help more than three hundred slaves, including her parents, escape. These trips put Tubman in personal danger. If she had been captured, she could have been enslaved again, or she could have been prosecuted under the federal Fugitive Slave Act, which made it a crime to aid a runaway slave.

★ **MARGARET SANGER** (1879–1966) began her career as an obstetrical nurse in 1912 in New York City. In her work with the poor, she saw the problems created by unwanted pregnancies—poverty and high rates of infant and maternal deaths. She believed in the equality of women and men and believed that equality would not be realized until women had information about birth control. Although it was illegal in New York, in 1916 she opened a clinic to distribute birth control information and devices. Sanger was arrested and sent to prison, and her legal appeals brought publicity to her cause. She later promoted the passage of a law allowing doctors to give birth control information to their patients. In 1921, she founded the American Birth Control League, which later became the Planned Parenthood Federation of America, and was also instrumental in founding the International Planned Parenthood Federation.

★ Attorney **THURGOOD MARSHALL** (1908–1993) worked for the National Association for the Advancement of Colored People (NAACP) from 1938 to 1961. He represented the NAACP before the Supreme Court in 1954 in *Brown vs. the Board of Education of Topeka*. He argued that "separate but equal" was unconstitutional under the Fourteenth Amendment, and the Court agreed with him unanimously. That decision ended racial segregation in the public schools of America. President Lyndon Johnson appointed Marshall to the Supreme Court. The first African American justice, Thurgood Marshall served from 1967 until his retirement in 1991.

★ In 1955, **ROSA PARKS** (1913–2005), an African American civil rights activist, refused to give up her seat on a public bus to a white man in Montgomery, Alabama. She was arrested for refusing to move to the back of the bus and was fined fourteen dollars. Her act of civil disobedience sparked the Montgomery Bus Boycott led by Martin Luther King Jr. Blacks in Montgomery boycotted buses for more than a year. In 1956, the U.S. Supreme Court declared segregated seating on the city's buses unconstitutional. The boycott ended, but its success encouraged other protests demanding civil rights for blacks.

★ CÉSAR CHÁVEZ (1927–1993) was awarded the Presidential Medal of Freedom posthumously in 1994 in recognition of his nonviolent activism and support of working people. A labor organizer, he started the National Farm Workers Association, which later became the United Farm Workers. He led strikes and successful nationwide boycotts of grapes and lettuce to win better working conditions for field workers. His

birthday, March 31, has become a holiday in a growing number of states.

★ DR. MARTIN LUTHER KING JR. (1929–1968), an African American Baptist minister, was a leader of the civil rights movement from 1955 until his assassination in 1968, when he was just thirty-nine years of age. He was instrumental in establishing the Southern Christian Leadership Conference, which promoted the right to vote for blacks and nonviolent demonstrations to protest racial discrimination. A powerful and charismatic orator, King delivered his "I have a dream" speech from the steps of the Lincoln Memorial on August 28, 1963, to more than 220,000 civil rights supporters. Many scholars rank that oration as the most important American speech of the twentieth century. His efforts helped lead to the passing of the Civil Rights Act of 1964 and the Voting Rights Act of 1965. He received the 1964 Nobel Peace Prize. In 1983, Congress created a federal holiday—the third Monday in January—honoring Martin Luther King Jr. ★

CHAPTER 15

THE NAME IS THE GAME

ELBRIDGE GERRY (1744–1814), a vice president to James Madison, is the inspiration for a political term in our English language. In 1812, in an effort to sustain his party's power, Gerry, who was then governor of Massachusetts, divided that state into electoral districts with more regard to politics than to geographical reality.

To a drawing of one of the governor's manipulated districts, Gilbert Stuart—the same fellow who had painted the famous portrait of George Washington—added a head, eyes, wings, and claws. According to one version of the story, Stuart exclaimed about his creation, "That looks like a salamander!" "No," countered the editor of the newspaper in which the cartoon was to appear. "Better call it a Gerrymander!" The verb *gerrymander* (now lowercased and sounded with a soft *g*, even though

Gerry's name began with a hard *g*) is still used today to describe the shaping of electoral districts for political gain.

Thousands of common words in our language are born from proper names. These words often lose their reference to specific persons and become generic terms in our dictionaries; when they do, they usually shed their capital letters.

The Greeks had a word for people who live on in our everyday conversations—*eponymos,* from which we derive the word *eponym,* meaning "after or upon a name." Stories of the origins of words made from people or places, real or imaginary, are among the richest and most entertaining about our language. Here's a quiz in which you are asked to identify ten common words and the names of the immortal Americans from whom they derive.

1. SAMUEL AUGUSTUS _____ (1803–1870), a San Antonio rancher, acquired vast tracts of land and dabbled in cattle raising. When he neglected to brand the calves born into his herd, his neighbors began calling the unmarked offspring by his name. Today this word has come to designate any nonconformist.

2. _____, the name of a courageous Apache warrior chief (1829–1909), became a battle cry for World War II paratroopers.

3. AMELIA JENKS _____ (1818–1894) was an American feminist who helped publicize the once-fashionable puffy ladies drawers that seemed to bloom like linen flowers.

4. A century before Elvis Presley, the handsome face of Civil War general AMBROSE E. _____ (1824–1881) was adorned by luxuriant side-whiskers sweeping down from his ears to his clean-shaven chin.

5. A colorful plant characterized by scarlet leaves is especially popular at Christmastime. This plant takes its name from JOEL R. _____ (1779–1851), our first ambassador to Mexico, who introduced it to the United States from its native land south of our border.

6. SYLVESTER _____ (1794–1851), an American dietary reformer, donated the name of a cracker made of ground whole wheat flour to our language.

7. A children's nonalcoholic cocktail made from club soda, grenadine, and a maraschino cherry takes the name of _____ _____ (1928–), the most famous of all child movie stars.

8. In the heyday of the American cowboy, **JOHN B.** _____ (1830–1906) created a hat with a high crown to hold a cushion of warm air and a wide brim to deflect rain and snow. A trapper offered him a five-dollar gold piece for the hat, and he sold it to him right off his head. He knew he had a winner.

9. _____ **STRAUSS** (1829–1902) was a German-Jewish immigrant who founded the first company to manufacture blue jeans. In the California gold rush days, he invented work trousers with copper rivets at the corners of the pockets so that the pants would not tear when loaded with samples of ore. The trousers continue to feature the now-superfluous rivets, and young people go to extraordinary lengths to make a new pair look old and ratty.

10. For the 1893 Chicago World's Fair, **GEORGE WASHINGTON GALE** _____ (1859–1896) built a great wheel. It revolved on a stationary axle, stood 264 feet high, and carried thirty-six cars, each capable of seating sixty people. While few wheels that came after have matched the grandeur of the prototype, the attraction dominates almost every amusement park and carnival. ★

Answers

1. maverick—Maverick ★ 2. geronimo!—Geronimo ★ 3. bloomers—Bloomer ★ 4. sideburns—Burnside ★ 5. poinsettia—Poinsett ★ 6. graham cracker—Graham ★ 7. Shirley Temple—Shirley Temple ★ 8. Stetson—Stetson ★ 9. levis—Levi ★ 10. Ferris wheel—Ferris

CHAPTER 16

AMERICA: THE MOTHER OF INVENTION

TINKERING IS A TIME-HONORED American pastime. Many men and women can't leave well enough alone. They're always trying to create something or improve something. As with most creative people, they benefit from the work of those who came before them, but they add that little spark of genius that can take their invention figuratively or literally into the stratosphere. Here are some of our best:

★ Among his many other talents as scientist, statesman, and publisher, **BENJAMIN FRANKLIN** (1706–1790) is the best known of our early inventors. We today are still nourished by the fruits of his fertile brain. He worked out the theory of the lightning rod during his study of electricity. His

Benjamin Franklin was one of America's greatest early inventors.

neighbors saw its practicality one night when lightning struck his house without causing damage. He created the Franklin stove that fit into a fireplace and gave off four times as much heat as the standard fireplace, with half the fuel. In his old age, Franklin tired of fumbling for his pairs of glasses, so he invented bifocals. For a century after their invention, they were called

Franklin spectacles. He also invented the odometer; the first flexible urinary catheter; and the claw pole, used to reach and grasp merchandise on high shelves. Most remarkably, Franklin refused to patent any of his inventions, preferring to have them used freely as his contribution to the general good. He understood that each invention built a foundation for something better. When he was in Paris and observed the first successful balloon flight in 1783, someone asked, "What good is it?" Franklin answered, "What good is a newborn baby?"

★ American presidents get in on the act of inventing: **THOMAS JEFFERSON** (1743–1826) invented a collapsible writing table and a pedometer to measure his walks, but **ABRAHAM LINCOLN** (1809–1865) was the only president to be awarded a patent, for a system of buoying vessels over shoals.

★ In 1793, **ELI WHITNEY** (1765–1825) invented the cotton gin, a machine that separated seeds from short-staple cotton fibers. Previously that had to be done by hand. One person could clean about one pound of cotton in a day; the gin could clean fifty pounds a day. Whitney's cotton gin helped the South become prosperous and the United States become the world's leading cotton grower. Whitney didn't make much money from the cotton gin, but he prospered as a New England gun manufacturer. He took a contract from the federal government

Robert Fulton made a living as an artist for several years before turning to engineering and invention.

to supply 10,000 muskets in two years. He accomplished this by building machines that would make standard interchangeable parts, a relatively new concept.

★ **ROBERT FULTON** (1765–1815) tried several different careers, including fine art, before he settled on being an engineer and inventor. He designed and built new types of canal boats, a machine for making rope, another for spinning flax, a dredging machine, and even a submarine. However, his greatest fame came from the *Clermont,* the first commercially successful steamboat. The *Clermont* began its first trip, from New York City up the Hudson River to Albany, on August 17, 1807, cutting the usual travel time from sixty-four hours to thirty-two hours for the 150-mile trip. It soon began regular passenger service.

★ Trained as an artist, **SAMUEL F. B. MORSE** (1791–1872) turned to invention as a career. It took him five years to achieve his first big success: he invented the telegraph and created

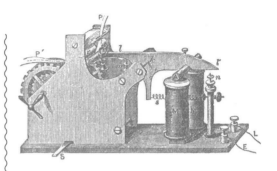

Samuel Morse's telegraph.

Morse code. In 1844 he built a test line between Baltimore and Washington, D.C., and tapped out the message, "What hath God wrought!" a sentence from biblical Numbers 23:23. In later life, he returned to art as the vice president of the new Metropolitan Museum of Art in New York.

★ **ALEXANDER GRAHAM BELL** (1847–1922), a teacher of the deaf, came to the United States from Scotland in 1871. He patented the first telephone in 1876. The first telephone exchange started in New Haven, Connecticut in 1878 with twenty-one customers. By 1880 there were fifty thousand telephones in the United States, and by

Alexander Graham Bell was a teacher of the deaf before inventing the telephone.

1900, one million. A transcontinental telephone line was completed in 1914, and on January 25, 1915, Bell placed the first transcontinental telephone call. He was in New York City when he called his close friend and assistant, Thomas A. Watson, in San Francisco. Watson was the same man who had answered Bell's very first telephone call in 1876. Bell had said, "Mister Watson, come here. I want you."

★ **THOMAS EDISON** (1847–1931) is the world's most famous and prolific inventor, one who followed his own motto: "Genius is one percent inspiration and ninety-nine percent perspiration." His greatest invention may have been the invention factory. Known as the Wizard of Menlo Park, he created the first modern industrial research laboratory and worked ceaselessly to develop or improve many products. Edison's invention of the light bulb transformed America and the world. He also had a hand in the invention of the phonograph, the mimeograph, and the Dictaphone, and improved

Known as the Wizard of Menlo Park, Thomas Edison held 1,093 U.S. patents.

the telegraph, telephone, and motion picture projector. Edison may not have invented the kitchen sink, but he seems to have invented everything else. He held a record 1,093 U.S. patents and thousands of patents in other countries. A canny businessman, he found financial partners worldwide and created new companies to manufacture and sell his products. After he invented the light bulb, he worked to create central power plants so that people would have power to light the bulbs. On September 4, 1882, his Edison Illuminating Company opened Pearl Street Station in New York City, the first electrical generating plant in the world. It produced four hundred amps and served eighty-five customers.

★ **GEORGE WASHINGTON CARVER** (1864?–1943) was born a slave. In 1896, he took a job working for Booker T. Washington as director of agricultural research at Tuskegee Institute (now Tuskegee University) in Alabama. He recognized that cotton, up until then the main crop of the South, was depleting the soil and that farmers needed profitable crops to substitute for cotton. Carver worked to develop products made from sweet potatoes, peanuts, and other crops, and ultimately developed 118 products from sweet potatoes and 300 from peanuts. By 1940, peanuts were the South's second largest cash crop.

★ Two wrongs don't make a right, but two Wrights did make an airplane. The **WRIGHT** brothers—**WILBUR** (1867–1912) and **ORVILLE** (1871–1948)—became interested in flight when, in 1896, they read of the death of glider pioneer Otto Lilienthal. The brothers

The Wright brothers' first flight at Kitty Hawk lasted only twelve seconds.

began by designing, building, and flying gliders. Testing models in a homebuilt wind tunnel, they created the first reliable tables of air pressures on curved surfaces. Wilbur and Orville became skilled pilots, and using their extensive knowledge, designed and built a powered airplane. On December 17, 1903, Orville made the first controlled flight of a heavier-than-air machine near Kitty Hawk, North Carolina, a 120-foot trip that lasted all of twelve seconds. The top speed was seven miles per hour and the highest altitude ten feet. Several years passed before their accomplishments became generally known. They spent the rest of their lives designing and flying planes and teaching others to fly.

★ In 1915, **CLARENCE BIRDSEYE** (1886–1956) went on a fur-trading and fishing trip to Labrador. Watching the Inuit freeze fish and caribou meat, he noted that quickly frozen food was fresher, better textured, and more flavorful than food that had been slowly frozen. In 1925, Birdseye developed a process for flash freezing small packages of food.

The Postum Cereal Company (later General Foods Corporation) purchased his patents in 1929. Frozen foods became popular in the 1950s, when freezers became widely available, and TV dinners took over living rooms.

★ **PHILO T. FARNSWORTH** (1906–1971) is credited with the invention of electronic television, although scientists all over the world were attempting to transmit pictures, the next logical step after transmitting words and voices. In 1927, Farnsworth's image dissector camera sent the first visual, a simple straight line. He continued working on the technology of television and ultimately was granted more than 150 U.S. patents. In 1936, NBC began experimental broadcasting with a telecast of a cartoon of Felix the Cat as its first program. Commercial TV began broadcasting on July 1, 1941, but was suspended for the duration of World War II. By 1950, three million TV sets had been sold. Today, more than 99 percent of American homes have televisions, most more than one. ★

CHAPTER 17

HOMEGROWN AUTHORS

ON THE NIGHT OF APRIL 20, 1910, Halley's Comet shone in the skies as it made its closest approach to the earth. Just a year before, **MARK TWAIN** said to a friend: "I came in with Halley's Comet in 1835. It is coming again next year, and I expect to go out with it. . . . The almighty has said, no doubt, 'Now here go these two unaccountable frauds; they came in together, they must go out together.' Oh! I am looking forward to that." On April 21, 1910, Mark Twain, the most American of American writers, did indeed go out with Halley's Comet.

HENRY DAVID THOREAU, who wrote *Walden,* helped runaway slaves escape to Canada and became one of the first Americans to speak in defense of radical abolitionist and outlaw John Brown. When Thoreau spent a day in jail for acting on the dictates of his conscience,

he was visited by friend **RALPH WALDO EMERSON.**

Emerson asked, "Henry, why are you here?"

Thoreau answered, "Waldo, why are you *not* here?"

Through biographical incidents, we can sometimes catch and crystallize the essence of a person's character. Here are some revealing episodes from the lives of a dozen famous American authors, each of whom you are asked to identify:

1. President Abraham Lincoln took this abolitionist author of *Uncle Tom's Cabin* by the hand and said, "So this is the little lady who made this big war."

2. When the first edition of this American poet's collection of poems appeared in 1855, the *Boston Intelligencer* said in its review: "The author should be kicked out from all decent society as below the level of the brute. He must be some escaped lunatic raving in pitiable delirium." The collection went through nine more editions and gained a large, enthusiastic readership in the United States and England.

3. Only seven of this New England woman's poems were published during her lifetime, and she left instructions that all her manuscripts be destroyed. Today she and her contemporary in the question above are the two most widely read and influential American poets of the nineteenth century.

4. This writer, critic, and humorist once arrived simultaneously at a narrow doorway with the playwright, journalist, and politician Clare Boothe Luce.

"Age before beauty," said Mrs. Luce, stepping aside.

"Pearls before swine," purred our writer as she glided through the doorway.

5. As a young cadet, this American writer was expelled from West Point for reporting to a march wearing nothing but white gloves. His epitaph reads, "Quoth the Raven, 'Nevermore,'" a line in his most famous poem.

6,7. When a popular Jazz Age American novelist remarked to another famous writer that "the rich are very different from you and me," the latter replied, "Yes, they have more money." Name the two authors.

8. When he was a young busboy in a Washington, D. C., hotel, this American poet left a packet of his poems next to the poet Vachel Lindsay's plate. Lindsay helped to launch the young man's career, and the busboy became the leading figure in the Harlem Renaissance.

9. In 1900, this author sat down to write a children's book about a girl named Dorothy, who was swept away to a fantastic land inhabited by munchkins, witches, a scarecrow, a tin man, and a lion. The fairy tale began as a bedtime story for the author's children and their friends and soon spilled over into several evening sessions. During one of the tellings, the author was asked the name of the strange place to which Dorothy was swept away. Glancing about the room, his eyes fell upon the drawers of a filing cabinet labeled "A–N" and "O–Z." Noting that the letters on the second label spelled out the *ah*s uttered by his rapt listeners, he named his fantastic land Oz.

10. This reclusive American writer was depicted in W. P. Kinsella's novel *Shoeless Joe.* When the subject threatened to sue, he was replaced in the film version, titled *Field of Dreams,* by a fictitious writer named Terence Mann, portrayed by James Earl Jones.

11. This American poet was asked to compose a poem and read it at John F. Kennedy's inauguration in 1961. When the sun's glare prevented him from reading the poem at the occasion, he instead recited his poem "The Gift Outright" from memory.

12. The publishers of the children's classic *Charlotte's Web* persuaded its author to record his book on tape. So caught had he become in the web of his arachnid heroine's life that it took nineteen tapings before the author could read aloud the passage about Charlotte's death without his voice cracking. ★

Answers

1. Harriet Beecher Stowe ★ 2. Walt Whitman ★ 3. Emily Dickinson ★ 4. Dorothy Parker ★ 5. Edgar Allan Poe ★ 6 and 7. F. Scott Fitzgerald and Ernest Hemingway ★ 8. Langston Hughes ★ 9. L. Frank Baum ★ 10. J. D. Salinger ★ 11. Robert Frost ★ 12. E. B. White

★ ★ ★ ★

PART 4

This American Language

★ ★ ★ ★

CHAPTER 18

A DECLARATION OF LANGUAGE INDEPENDENCE

BEGINNING WITH THE PILGRIMS, the story of language in America is the story of our Declaration of Linguistic Independence, the separating from its parent of that magnificent upstart we call American English.

JOHN ADAMS was one of the first to lead the charge for American linguistic autonomy. In 1780, sixteen years before he became president, he called upon Congress to establish an academy for "correcting, improving, and ascertaining the English language." "English," Adams proclaimed, "is destined to be in the next and succeeding centuries more generally the language of the world than Latin was in the last or French is in the present age.

The reason of this is obvious, because the increasing population in America, and their universal connection and correspondence with all nations, will, aided by the influence of England in the world, whether great or small, force their language into general use."

At the time Adams made that prediction, an obscure Connecticut schoolmaster was soon to become a one-man academy of American English. His name, now synonymous with the word *dictionary,* was Webster. **NOAH WEBSTER** (1758–1843) saw the untapped promise of the new republic. He was afire with the conviction that a United States no longer politically dependent on England should also become independent in language. In his *Dissertations on the English Language,* published in 1789, Webster declared linguistic war on the King's English: "As an independent nation, our honor requires us to have a system of our own, in language as well as government. Great Britain, whose children we are, and whose language we speak, should no longer be our standard; for the taste of her writers is already corrupted, and her language on the decline."

In putting his vision into practice, Noah Webster traveled throughout America, listening to people's speech and taking detailed notes. He included in his dictionaries an array of shiny new American words, among them *applesauce, bullfrog, chowder, handy, hickory, succotash, tomahawk*—and *skunk:* "a quadruped remarkable for its smell." Webster also proudly used quotations by Americans to illustrate and clarify many of his definitions. The likes of Ben Franklin, George Washington, John Jay, and Washington Irving took their places as authorities alongside William Shakespeare, John Milton, and the Bible. In shaping the American language, Webster also taught a new nation a new way to spell. He deleted the *u* from words such as *honour* and *labour* and the *k* from words such as *musick* and *publick,* he reversed the last two letters in words such as *centre* and *theatre,* and he Americanized the spelling of words such as *plough* and *gaol.*

Perhaps no one has celebrated this "American dialect" with more passion and vigor than the poet **WALT WHITMAN.** "The Americans are going to be the most fluent and melodious-voiced people in the world—and the most perfect users of words," he predicted before the Civil War. "The new world, the new times, the new people, the new vistas need a new tongue. What is more, they will . . . not be satisfied until it is evolved."

More than a century later, it's debatable whether Americans are "the most fluent and melodious-voiced people in the world," but there is no question that we are still engaged in the American Evolution and that our American parlance is as rollicking and pyrotechnic as ever. Consider our invention, in the past fifty years, of delectables on the order of *carbon footprint, couch potato, mouse potato* (a couch potato attached to a computer), *digerati, hottie, humongous, ginormous, slam dunk, sleazebag, soccer mom,* and *unfriend.*

"IN AMERICA THERE IS MORE SPACE WHERE NOBODY IS THAN WHERE ANYBODY IS. THIS IS WHAT MAKES AMERICA WHAT IT IS."—*Gertrude Stein*

Walt Whitman was a passionate proponent of the new "American dialect."

From the early 1700s, the British have thundered against what one of their magazines called "the torrent of barbarous phraseology" that poured from the American colonies. The first British broadside launched against an Americanism is recorded in 1735, when an English visitor named Francis Moore referred to the young city of Savannah as standing upon a hill overlooking a river "which they in barbarous English call a bluff."

The British were still beating their breasts over what the *Monthly Mirror* called "the corruptions and barbarisms which are hourly obtaining in the speech of our trans-Atlantic colonies," long after we stopped being colonies. They objected to almost every term that they did not consider standard English, protesting President Jefferson's use of the verb *belittle*. They expressed shock at the

"AMERICA. IT IS A FABULOUS COUNTRY, THE ONLY FABULOUS COUNTRY. IT IS THE ONLY PLACE WHERE MIRACLES NOT ONLY HAPPEN, BUT WHERE THEY HAPPEN ALL THE TIME."—*Thomas Wolfe*

American tendency to employ, in place of *suppose,* the likes of *expect, reckon, calculate,* and—a special target—*guess,* conveniently overlooking Geoffrey Chaucer's centuries-old "Of twenty yeer of age he was, I gesse."

Returning from a tour through the United States in the late nineteenth century, the playwright Oscar Wilde jested, "We really have everything in common with America nowadays except, of course, language." Wilde's fellow playwright George Bernard Shaw observed,

"England and America are two countries separated by a common language."

But our homegrown treasure Mark Twain put it all into perspective when he opined about American English, as compared with British English: "The property has gone into the hands of a joint stock company, and we own the bulk of the shares." ★

Mark Twain was perhaps the most American of American authors.

CHAPTER 19

TALKING TURKEY

AS THE (PROBABLY APOCRYPHAL) TALE spins out, back in the early colonial days, a white hunter and a friendly Native American made a pact before they started out on the day's hunt. Whatever they bagged was to be divided equally between them. At the end of the day, the white man undertook to distribute the spoils, consisting of several buzzards and turkeys. He suggested to his fellow hunter, "Either I take the turkeys and you the buzzards, or you take the buzzards and I take the turkeys." At this point the Native American complained, "You talk buzzard to me. Now talk turkey." And ever since, *to talk turkey* has meant "to tell it like it is."

Let's talk turkey about our Native American heritage. Suppose you had been one of the early explorers or settlers of North America. You would have found many things in your new land unknown to you. The handiest way of filling voids in your vocabulary would have been to ask local Native Americans what words they used. The early colonists began borrowing words from friendly Indians almost from the moment of their first contact, and many of those names have remained in our everyday language:

"I HAVE FALLEN IN LOVE WITH AMERICAN NAMES, THE SHARP, GAUNT NAMES THAT NEVER GET FAT."—*Stephen Vincent Benet*

FOOD: *squash* (Narraganset), *pecan* (Algonquian), *hominy* (Algonquian), *pone* (Algonquian), *pemmican* (Cree), and *succotash* (Narraganset).

PEOPLE: *sachem* (Narraganset), *squaw* (Massachuset), *papoose* (Narraganset), and *mugwump* (Natick).

DAILY LIFE: *moccasin* (Chippewa), *toboggan* (Algonquian), *tomahawk* (Algonquian), *wigwam* (Abenaki), *teepee* (Dakota), *caucus* (Algonquian), *powwow* (Narraganset or Massachuset), *wampum* (Massachuset), *bayou* (Choctaw), *potlatch* (Chinook), *hogan* (Navajo), *hickory* (Algonquian), *kayak* (Inuit), *parka* (Aleut), and *totem* (Ojibwa).

Pronouncing many of the Native American words was difficult for the early explorers and settlers. In many instances, they had to shorten and simplify the names. Given the Native American names, identify the following animals: *apossoun, otchock, rahaugcum,* and *segankw.*

A squaw *and her* papoose.

The word chipmunk *comes from the Ojibwa people of the Great Lakes region.*

The animals are: *opossum* (Algonquian), *woodchuck* (Narraganset), *raccoon* (Algonquian), and *skunk* (Algonquian). To this menagerie we may add the likes of *caribou* (Micmac), *chipmunk* (Ojibwa), *moose* (Algonquian), *muskrat* (Abenaki), and *porgy* (Algonquian).

If you look at a map of the United States, you will realize how freely settlers used words of Indian origin to name the places where we live. Rivers, lakes, ponds, creeks, mountains, valleys, counties, towns, and cities as large as Chicago (from a Fox word that means "place that stinks of onions" or from another Indian word that means "great, powerful") bear Native American names. Four of our five Great Lakes—Huron, Ontario, Michigan, and Erie—and twenty-five of our states have names that were borrowed from Native American words:

ALABAMA: name of a tribe in the Creek Confederacy

ALASKA: mainland (Aleut)

ARIZONA: place of the little springs (Papago)

ARKANSAS: downstream people (Sioux)

CONNECTICUT: place of the long river (Algonquian)

IDAHO: behold the sun coming down the mountains (Shoshone)

ILLINOIS: superior people (Illini)

"AMERICA IS A LAND OF WONDERS, IN WHICH EVERYTHING IS IN CONSTANT MOTION AND EVERY CHANGE SEEMS AN IMPROVEMENT. NO NATURAL BOUNDARY SEEMS TO BE SET TO THE EFFORTS OF MAN; AND IN HIS EYES WHAT IS NOT YET DONE IS ONLY WHAT HE HAS NOT YET ATTEMPTED TO DO."—*Alexis de Tocqueville*

IOWA: beautiful land (Ioway)
KANSAS: south wind people (Sioux)
KENTUCKY: meadowland (Cherokee)
MASSACHUSETTS: great hill place (Massachuset)
MICHIGAN: great water (Chippewa)
Minnesota: milky blue water (Sioux)
MISSISSIPPI: father of waters (Ojibwa)
MISSOURI: people of the large canoes (Fox)
NEBRASKA: flat water (Sioux)
NORTH DAKOTA and **SOUTH DAKOTA:** named for the Dakota tribe
OHIO: great river (Iroquois)
OKLAHOMA: red people (Choctaw)
TENNESSEE: name of a Cherokee village
TEXAS: friends (Tejas)
UTAH: name of a Ute tribe
WISCONSIN: gathering of waters (Algonquian)
WYOMING: large prairie place (Delaware)

Some of our loveliest place names began life as Native American words—Susquehanna, Shenandoah, Rappahannock. Such names are the stuff of poetry. To the poet Walt Whitman, Monongahela "rolls with venison richness upon the palate." William Penn wrote about the Leni-Lenape Indians: "I know not a language spoken in Europe that hath words of more sweetness and greatness." How fortunate we are that the poetry the First Peoples heard in the American landscape lives on in our American language. ★

CHAPTER 20

ALL-AMERICAN DIALECTS

FROM CALIFORNIA TO THE NEW YORK island, from the redwood forest to the Gulf Stream waters, we hear America singing. We are teeming nations within a nation, a nation that is like a world. We talk in melodies of infinite variety; we dance to their sundry measures and lyrics.

Midway through John Steinbeck's epic novel *The Grapes of Wrath,* young Ivy observes, "Ever'body says words different. Arkansas folks says 'em different, and Oklahomy folks says 'em different. And we seen a lady from Massachusetts, an' she said 'em differentest of all. Couldn't hardly make out what she was sayin'."

One aspect of American rugged individualism is that not all of us say the same word in the same way. Sometimes we don't even use the same name for the same object.

I (coauthor Richard Lederer) was born and grew up in Philadelphia a coon's age, a blue moon, and a month of Sundays ago, when Hector was a pup. *Phillufia,* or *Philly,* which is what we kids called the city, was where the Epicurean delight made with cold cuts, cheese, tomatoes, lettuce, pickles, and onions stuffed into a long, hard-crusted Italian bread loaf was invented.

The creation of that sandwich took place in the Italian pushcart section of the city, known as Hog Island. Some linguists contend that it was but a short leap from *Hog Island* to *hoagie,* while others claim that the label *hoagie* arose because only a

"THE AMERICAN EXPERIMENT IS THE MOST TREMENDOUS AND FAR-REACHING ENGINE OF SOCIAL CHANGE WHICH HAS EVER EITHER BLESSED OR CURSED MANKIND."
—*Charles Francis Adams*

hog had the appetite or the technique to eat one properly.

As a young adult I moved to northern New England (*N'Hampsha,* to be specific), where the same sandwich designed to be a meal in itself is called a grinder—because you need a good set of grinders to chew it. But my travels around the United States have revealed that the hoagie or grinder is called at least a dozen other names—a bomber, Garibaldi (after the Italian liberator), hero, Italian sandwich, rocket, sub, submarine (which is what they call it in California, where I now live), torpedo, wedge, wedgie, and, in the deep South, a poor-boy (usually pronounced *poh-boy*).

In Philadelphia, we wash our hoagies down with soda. In New England we do it with tonic, and by that word I don't mean medicine. Soda and tonic in other parts are known as pop, soda pop, soft drink, Coke, and quinine.

In northern New England, they take the term *milk shake* quite literally. To many residing in that little corner of the country, a milk shake consists of milk mixed with flavored syrup—and nothing more—shaken up until foamy. If you live in Rhode Island or in southern Massachusetts and you want ice cream in your milk drink, you ask for a cabinet (named after the square wooden cabinet in which the mixer was encased). If you live farther north, you order a velvet or a frappe (from the French *frapper,* "to ice").

Clear—or is it clean?—or is it plumb?—across the nation, Americans sure do talk "different."

What do you call those flat, doughy things you often eat for breakfast—battercakes, flannel cakes, flapjacks, griddle cakes, or pancakes?

Is that simple strip of grass between the street and the sidewalk a berm, boulevard, boulevard strip, city strip, devil strip, green belt, the parking, parking strip, parkway, sidewalk plot, strip, swale, tree bank, or tree lawn?

Battercakes, flannel cakes, flapjacks, griddle cakes, or pancakes?

Is the part of the highway that separates the northbound lanes from the southbound lanes the center strip, mall, medial strip, median strip, medium strip, or neutral ground?

Is it a cock horse, dandle, hicky horse, horse, horse tilt, ridy horse, seesaw, teeter, teeterboard, teetering board, teetering horse, teeter-totter, tilt, tilting board, tinter, tinter board, or tippity bounce?

Do fisherpersons employ an angledog, angleworm, baitworm, earthworm, eaceworm, fishworm, mudworm, rainworm, or redworm? Is a larger worm a dew worm, night crawler, night walker, or town worm?

Is it a crabfish, clawfish, craw, crawdab, crawdad, crawdaddy, crawfish, crawler, crayfish, creekcrab, crowfish, freshwater lobster, ghost shrimp, mudbug, spiny lobster, or yabby?

Depends where you live and whom it is you're talking to.

"THIS IS AMERICA . . . A BRILLIANT DIVERSITY SPREAD LIKE STARS, LIKE A THOUSAND POINTS OF LIGHT IN A BROAD AND PEACEFUL SKY."
—George H. W. Bush

We figger, figure, guess, imagine, opine, reckon, and suspect that our being bull-headed, contrary, headstrong, muley, mulish, ornery, otsny, pigheaded, set, sot, stubborn, or utsy about this whole matter of dialects makes you sick to, in, or at your stomach.

But we assure you that, when it comes to American dialects, we're not speaking flapdoodle, flumaddiddle, flummydiddle, or flurriddiddle. We're no all-thumbs-and-no-fingers, all-knees-and-elbows, all-left-feet, all-hat-and-no-cattle, antigoddling, bumfuzzled, discombobulated, frustrated, foozled bumpkin, clodhopper, country jake, hayseed, hick, hillbilly, Hoosier, jackpine savage, mossback, mountain-boomer, pumpkin-husker, rail-splitter, rube, sodbuster, stump farmer, swamp angel, yahoo, or yokel.

If you ask most adults what a dialect is, they will tell you it's what somebody else in another region passes off as English. These regions tend to be exotic places like Mississippi or Texas—or Brooklyn, where *oil* is a rank of nobility and *earl* is a black, sticky substance.

If the truth be told, we all have accents. Many New Englanders drop the *r* in *cart* and *farm* and say *caht* and *fahm.* Thus the Midwesterner's "park the car in Harvard

On the farm *or the* fahm?
Depends on where you live.

Yard" becomes the New Englander's "pahk the cah in Hahvahd Yahd." But those *r*'s aren't lost. A number of upper-class Northeasterners add *r*'s to words, such as *idear* and *Chiner* when those words come before a vowel or at the end of a sentence.

The most widespread of American dialects is that spoken across the South. It's reported that many Southerners reacted to the elections of Jimmy Carter and Bill Clinton by saying, "Well, at last we have a president who talks without an accent." Actually, Southerners, like everyone else, do speak with an accent, as witness these tongue-in-cheek entries in "A Dictionary of Southernisms":

AH: organ for seeing

ARE: sixty minutes

ARN: ferrous metal

ASS: frozen water

AST: questioned

BANE: small, kidney-shaped vegetable

BAR: seek and receive a loan; a grizzly

BOLD: heated in water

CARD: one who lacks courage

FARST: a lot of trees

FUR: distance

HAR: to employ

HEP: to assist

HIRE YEW: a greeting

PAW TREE: verse

RAT: opposite of *left*

RATS: what the Constitution guarantees us

RECKANIZE: to see

RETARD: stopped working at the job

SEED: past tense of *saw*

TAR: a rubber wheel

TARRED: exhausted

T'MAR: day following *t'day*

THANG: item

THANK: to cogitate

Y'ALL: a bunch of *you's*

Each language is a great pie. Each slice of that pie is a dialect, and no single slice is the language.

In the early 1960s, John Steinbeck decided to rediscover America in a camper with his French poodle, Charley. The writer reported his observations in *Travels with Charley* and included these thoughts on American dialects:

"THERE IS NOTHING WRONG WITH AMERICA THAT CANNOT BE CURED BY WHAT IS RIGHT WITH AMERICA."—*Bill Clinton*

One of my purposes was to listen, to hear speech, accent, speech rhythms, overtones, and emphasis. For speech is so much more than words and sentences. I did listen everywhere. It seemed to me that regional speech is in the process of disappearing, not gone but going. Forty years of radio and twenty years of television must have this impact. Communications must destroy localness by a slow, inevitable process.

I can remember a time when I could almost pinpoint a man's place of origin by his speech. That is growing more difficult now and will in some foreseeable future become impossible. It is a rare house or building that is not rigged with spiky combers of the air. Radio and television speech becomes standardized, perhaps better English than we have ever used. Just as our *bread, mixed and baked, packaged and sold without benefit of accident or human frailty, is uniformly good and uniformly tasteless, so will our speech become one speech.*

More than a half century has passed since Steinbeck made that observation, and the hum and buzz of electronic voices have since permeated almost every home across our nation. Formerly, the psalmist tells us, "The voice of the turtle was heard in the land." Now it is the voice of the broadcaster, with his or her immaculately groomed diction. Let us hope that American English does not turn into a bland, homogenized, pasteurized, assembly-line product. May our bodacious American English remain tasty and nourishing—full of flavor, variety, and local ingredients. ★

★ ★ ★ ★

PART 5

This Land Is Our Land

★ ★ ★ ★

CHAPTER 21

AMERICA THE BEAUTIFUL

MANY AMERICANS travel all over the world searching for beauty, when it exists in their own backyards. Join us for a tour of our homegrown American beauties.

★ UNESCO has designated Cahokia Mounds State Historic Site in Illinois as one of twenty-one **WORLD HERITAGE SITES** in the United States. Cahokia Mounds covers four thousand acres and is the largest archeological site in the United States. Its most striking feature is Monks Mound, which covers almost fourteen acres and required twenty-two million cubic feet of soil to construct. Cahokia, an Indian city in southern Illinois, was occupied from AD 700. It flowered between 1050 and 1200 with 10,000 to 20,000 inhabitants. At its height, it was larger than London was at the time. It was abandoned by 1400, possibly because of a change in weather that made farming unproductive.

In addition to Cahokia Mounds, the other U.S. World Heritage Sites are:

- Carlsbad Caverns National Park, New Mexico
- Chaco Culture National Historical Park, New Mexico
- Everglades National Park, Florida
- Grand Canyon National Park, Arizona
- Great Smoky Mountains National Park, Tennessee and North Carolina
- Hawaii Volcanoes National Park, Hawaii
- Independence Hall, Pennsylvania
- Wrangell-St. Elias National Park and Preserve, and Glacier Bay National Park and Preserve, Alaska (along with neighboring Kluane National Park and Reserve, and Tatshenshini-Alsek National Park, Canada)
- La Fortaleza and San Juan National Historic Site, Puerto Rico

"FOR OTHER NATIONS, UTOPIA IS A BLESSED PAST NEVER TO BE RECOVERED; FOR AMERICANS IT IS JUST BEYOND THE HORIZON."
—Henry Kissinger

- Mammoth Cave National Park, Kentucky
- Mesa Verde National Park, Colorado
- Monticello/University of Virginia, Virginia
- Olympic National Park, Washington
- Papahānaumokuākea Marine National Monument (a linear cluster of small, low-lying islands and atolls northeast of Hawaii)
- Pueblo de Taos National Historic Landmark, New Mexico
- Redwood National and State Parks, California
- Statue of Liberty National Monument, New York
- Waterton-Glacier International Peace Park, Montana (and Canada)
- Yellowstone National Park, Wyoming, Idaho, and Montana
- Yosemite National Park, California

★ The United States has coastlines on three oceans—the Atlantic, the Pacific, and the Arctic. The United States, Canada, Denmark, Norway, and Russia are competing to establish claims to Arctic land exposed by the retreat of northern glaciers.

★ Canada and the United States share **LAKE SUPERIOR**, the largest body of fresh water in the world.

★ **CRATER LAKE** in southern Oregon is the deepest lake in the United States and the seventh deepest in the world. It sits in the caldera of Mount Mazama, an extinct volcano. It was measured by multibeam side-scan sonar in 2000 and was

*Mount McKinley's Athabascan name,
Denali, means "the high one."*

found to be 1,949 feet deep. It's fed only
by rainwater and snowmelt, so it's also
one of the clearest lakes in the world.

★ **YOSEMITE FALLS** in Yosemite National
Park, at 2,425 feet high, is the highest
waterfall in North America and the
seventh highest in the world.

★ **MINNESOTA** is called the "Land of
10,000 Lakes." In fact, the state contains more than 11,840 lakes that are
larger than ten acres.

★ The **GREAT SALT LAKE** in landlocked
Utah is the largest body of saltwater
in the United States. It's so salty that,
even in the coldest of Utah winters, it
has never frozen over.

★ **MOUNT MCKINLEY** in south central
Alaska, also known in the Athabascan
language as Denali, is the highest point
in North America at 20,320 feet. It's
named in honor of President William
McKinley.

★ Mount McKinley is dwarfed by
MAUNA KEA on the Big Island
of Hawaii. Only 13,796 feet high

measured from sea level, it's the tallest mountain on earth if measured from its base. At 33,476 feet, it's taller than Mount Everest (29,035 feet). Mauna Kea means "White Mountain," in reference to its wintertime snowy cap. Yes, snow in Hawaii. You can go skiing there. You can also see one of the world's largest groupings of optical telescopes, thirteen in all, including four of the most colossal telescopes in the world: Keck I, Keck II, Subaru, and Gemini North.

★ At 13,678 feet above sea level, Mauna Kea's companion, **MAUNA LOA** ("Long Mountain"), as measured from its base, is also taller than Mount Everest. It's the largest volcano in volume and area covered on the earth. Since 1832, it has erupted thirty-nine times.

★ The United States is one of the most volcanically active nations on the planet. The U.S. Geological Survey monitors 170 volcanoes in Alaska, Washington, Oregon, California, Arizona, New Mexico, Idaho, Wyoming, Hawaii, and the Mariana Islands. Volcanoes are considered active or potentially active if they have erupted in the last ten thousand years. **KILAUEA,** in Hawaii Volcanoes National Park, is the world's most active volcano, and the U.S. Geological Survey considers it the most dangerous volcano on earth. It's the home of Pele, the fire goddess. She lives in the world's largest volcanic crater, measuring three miles long by two miles wide by five hundred feet deep. While all other American coasts are eroding, the coastline of the Big Island of Hawaii is growing as lava flows into the sea from Kilauea.

★ At 2,323 miles long, the **MISSISSIPPI RIVER** is the largest river system in North America. Along with its major tributary, the Missouri River, it drains all or part of thirty-one states.

★ **DEATH VALLEY** features the lowest point in the United States, Badwater Basin, at 282 feet below sea level, and experienced the highest temperature ever recorded in our country, 134 degrees Fahrenheit, at Furnace Creek on July 10, 1913. Death Valley normally receives less than two inches of rain per year. Only eighty-five miles separate Badwater from the highest point in the contiguous forty-eight states—Mount Whitney, 14,505 feet above sea level.

★ The coldest temperature ever recorded in the United States was measured at **PROSPECT CREEK CAMP** in northern Alaska. On January 23, 1971, it was -79.8 degrees Fahrenheit.

★ **MOUNT WASHINGTON,** New Hampshire, may have the worst weather in our country. Winds routinely blow at a hundred miles per hour. A record gust was measured at 231 mph, the highest wind speed ever recorded in the United States.

★ At 750 feet, **STAR DUNE** is our nation's tallest sand dune. It can be found among the thirty square miles of dunes in Colorado's Great Sand Dunes National Park.

★ The catastrophic San Francisco earthquake of April 18, 1906, was estimated to register between 7.2 and 8.0 if it had been measured by the Richter Scale, which was not created until 1935, but there was likely an even more severe quake in the continental United States. On February 12, 1812, a quake struck near New Madrid, Missouri, one so powerful that it temporarily reversed the course of the Mississippi River. On March 27, 1964, a monster quake measuring 8.4 on the Richter Scale flattened the entire downtown business section of Anchorage, Alaska. That quake was the second strongest ever recorded by a seismograph. ★

At least 3,000 people were estimated to have died in the 1906 San Francisco earthquake.

CHAPTER 22

STATES OF THE UNION

AS A REWARD FOR READING this far in *American Trivia,* we, your intrepid coauthors, will now share with you a question guaranteed to stump almost all of your family and friends. Of our fifty states, which is the most northerly, which the most westerly, which the most easterly, and which the most southerly? The answers are: Alaska, Alaska, Alaska, and Hawaii. Here's why: Hawaii is more southerly than Florida, and Alaska is clearly our most northerly state. The Aleutian Islands, which are part of Alaska, arc about 1,110 miles west of the Alaskan Peninsula and cross the 180th meridian—the dividing line between the Eastern and Western hemispheres. That makes Alaska the state that's not just farthest north, but also the farthest west and farthest east.

We state that our states are unique and the state of our states amazing. Read on to see what we mean.

★ **ALASKA** was admitted as the forty-ninth state in January 1959, **HAWAII** as the fiftieth in August of the same year. The Hawaiian Islands and the western Aleutian Islands off Alaska share the same time zone.

★ The **NORTH SLOPE BOROUGH** in Alaska, home of the Inupiat Eskimos, is the largest county in the United States. It's the size of Wyoming. Barrow, its largest city, has a population of 4,500. The smallest and most densely populated county is New York County, which comprises primarily Manhattan Island. It's only 22.96 square miles, but it contains more than a million and a half denizens.

★ The coastline of **ALASKA** is longer than the entire coastline of the lower forty-eight states. Seventy-five New Jerseys could fit into Alaska. Alaska is not only our largest state, but is larger than the second and third largest states—Texas and California—combined. Taken together these three states make up more than a quarter of our nation's total acreage.

★ The original thirteen states, in roughly geographical order from north to south, were **NEW HAMPSHIRE, MASSACHUSETTS, RHODE ISLAND, CONNECTICUT, NEW YORK, NEW JERSEY, PENNSYLVANIA, DELAWARE, MARYLAND, VIRGINIA, NORTH CAROLINA, SOUTH CAROLINA,** and **GEORGIA.** Two of the New England states were not included: **VERMONT** was an independent republic between 1777 and 1791, when it became our fourteenth state, and **MAINE** was a district of Massachusetts until it became our twenty-third state in 1820.

★ **VIRGINIA** is the birth state of the greatest number of our presidents, including four of the first five and seven of the first twelve: George Washington, Thomas Jefferson, James Madison, James Monroe, William Henry Harrison, John Tyler, and Zachary Taylor, as well as twentieth-century president Woodrow Wilson. Jefferson, Monroe, and Tyler were also governors of Virginia.

★ In competition with Virginia, **OHIO** is known as the "Mother of Presidents" because eight American presidents came from there—William Henry Harrison, Ulysses S. Grant, Rutherford B. Hayes, James Garfield (Grant, Hayes, and Garfield served consecutively), Benjamin Harrison, William McKinley, William Howard Taft, and Warren G. Harding.

★ **KENTUCKY** gave birth to two presidents on opposite sides during the Civil War. The first president born outside of the original thirteen colonies, Abraham Lincoln began life in Hodgenville, Kentucky. Jefferson Davis, president of the Confederacy, was born in Christian County, Kentucky.

★ **IDAHO** and **HAWAII** are the only states never owned by a foreign nation. The

British established the original thirteen colonies. The French owned what later became the Louisiana Purchase. The Spanish owned Florida and the Southwest. The Russians owned Alaska, Washington, Oregon, and part of California. New Sweden was established in America in 1638, when Fort Christina was built where Wilmington, Delaware, is now situated. In 1655, New Sweden was captured and absorbed by the Dutch colony of New Amsterdam (later New York).

★ Some parts of the United States have been independent nations. One was the **VERMONT REPUBLIC,** mentioned above. **HAWAII** was an independent kingdom and then a republic before it was annexed as a territory in 1898. The **REPUBLIC OF TEXAS** existed from 1836 until 1845.

★ A number of other areas claimed nationhood, but were never recognized by the United States or any other governments. The largest of these was the **CONFEDERATE STATES OF AMERICA.**

> ## "DOUBLE—NO, TRIPLE— OUR TROUBLES, AND WE'D STILL BE BETTER OFF THAN ANY OTHER PEOPLE ON EARTH."
> *—Ronald Reagan*

But there were others. Part of what is now the state of Tennessee declared itself the **STATE OF FRANKLIN.** Native Americans in a part of Florida declared themselves to be citizens of the **STATE OF MUSKOGEE.** The **REPUBLIC OF WEST FLORIDA** claimed territory in Florida, Mississippi, Louisiana, and Alabama. New Hampshire was the home of the **REPUBLIC OF INDIAN STREAM.** Texas had the **REPUBLIC OF RIO GRANDE,** and California had the **CALIFORNIA REPUBLIC.**

★ In 1803, the United States completed the **LOUISIANA PURCHASE** from France for $15 million. It comprised what later became Iowa, North Dakota, South Dakota, Arkansas, Kansas, Louisiana,

THE
LOUISIANA
PURCHASE (1803)

MILES
100 50 0   100   200   300

Missouri, Nebraska, Oklahoma, Texas, and parts of Colorado, Minnesota, Montana, and Wyoming. The Louisiana Purchase was negotiated by James Monroe and Robert Livingston, Thomas Jefferson's diplomats to France. Although Monroe later became president of the United States, he always considered the Purchase to be his greatest achievement.

★ In 1840, the United States measured just under 1.7 million square miles. By the end of the decade, our nation had grown to 2.9 million square miles, vaster than all of Europe.

★ With the **GADSDEN PURCHASE** of 1853, the territory of the continental forty-eight states became complete. Arizona was the last continental state to be admitted to the Union, on Valentine's Day, February 14, 1912.

★ Part of the Louisiana Purchase was set aside as Indian Territory in 1828. By 1889, the government had displaced the Native Americans and opened the Indian lands of **OKLAHOMA** to settlers, who could each homestead 160 acres. On April 22, 1889, fifty thousand homesteading "Boomers" waited. At high noon, a bugle sounded and the land rush was on. That night, over ten thousand people lived in a tent city in Guthrie. Oklahoma City gained twenty-five thousand citizens in just a few hours. Sixty thousand people lived in Oklahoma by the end of the year. But some settlers and speculators had sneaked onto public land before the designated time and were thus called "Sooners," giving Oklahoma the nickname the "Sooner State."

★ The states that border the most other states—eight—are **TENNESSEE** and **MISSOURI. MAINE** is the only state that touches just one other state, **NEW HAMPSHIRE.** Only **ALASKA** and **HAWAII** stand alone.

★ **MICHIGAN** borders four of the five Great Lakes.

★ What state has the greatest percentage of its state boundary in shoreline? It's **HAWAII,** but few people will think of that answer.

★ **WASHINGTON** is the only state named after a president.

★ **NEW MEXICO** is the only state named after a foreign country.

★ One out of eight of us lives in **CALIFORNIA**; the second most populous state is **TEXAS.** These states will continue to attract people as the mean center of our population inexorably shifts southward and westward. The 2010 mean center of population is near the village of Plato in Texas County, Missouri. That center moved 23.4 miles southwest of where it had been in the year 2000. ★

CHAPTER 23

A LETTER-PERFECT QUIZ

WHAT IS THE ONLY LETTER that does not appear in the name of any state?

The answer is *q.*

Not counting Iowa and Utah, how many U.S. states have only four letters in their names?

The answer is seven! Look at the names *Alabama, Alaska, Hawaii, Indiana, Kansas, Mississippi,* and *Tennessee.* If you count the different letters that make up *Alabama,* there are only four: *A, L, B,* and *M.* The same trick works for the other state names we've just listed.

These are but two of the letter games you can play with stately words. Here are some other letter-perfect exotica of the states we're in:

★ *Arkansas* is the longest state name with only the one vowel *a* (*Alabama, Alaska,* and *Kansas* are the other three) and the only one-word state name within which appears a second state name, written solidly—*Kansas. West Virginia* is the only two-word state name with this characteristic.

★ What begins with a union and ends with a separation? The answer is *Connecticut,* which can be cleft into the oxymoron *Connect I cut.*

★ *Hawaii* is one of only two states with a double vowel. The other is *Tennessee. HAWAII* is also the longest state name whose capital letters are vertically symmetrical and will thus appear the same in a mirror. The other three are *IOWA, OHIO,* and *UTAH.* Finally, *Hawaii* is the only state whose capital alternates consonants and vowels—*Honolulu.*

★ *Iowa* is the only state besides *Ohio* that contains three syllables and only one consonant.

★ *Kentucky* is the only state whose name ends with its postal abbreviation.

★ *Louisiana* is the only state with *USA* inside its borders.

★ *Maine* is the only one-syllable state. Lop off the last letter and you have a homophone: *Maine/main.*

★ *Massachusetts* is, with thirteen letters, the longest single-word state name. *North* and *South Carolina* each match the length of *Massachusetts* in two words.

★ *Minnesota* yields the longest anagram of any state. That is, you can rearrange the letters in *Minnesota* and come up with *nominates.*

★ In letter patterning, *Mississippi* is clearly the best of the state names, rivaled only by *Tennessee.* Both names contain just one vowel repeated four times, three sets of double letters, and only four different letters. But *Mississippi* has the distinction of containing a seven-letter embedded palindrome—*ississi;* three overlapping four-letter palindromes—*issi, issi,* and *ippi;* and a double triple—*ississ.*

★ In addition to *Maine, Massachusetts,* and *Mississippi,* five other states begin with the popular letter *m: Maryland, Michigan, Minnesota, Missouri,* and *Montana.*

★ Four states are "new": *New Hampshire, New Jersey, New Mexico,* and *New York.*

★ How many states have capital cities that begin with the same letter as their state? The answer is four: *Dover, Delaware; Honolulu, Hawaii; Indianapolis, Indiana;* and *Oklahoma City, Oklahoma.*

★ *A* is the most frequently occurring letter in our state names, and twenty-one states end with that letter. The vowel *a* or the consonant *n,* or both, repose in forty-seven of our fifty states. The only three exceptions are *Mississippi, Missouri,* and *Ohio.*

★ A LETTER-PERFECT QUIZ ★

★ Within the borders of *New Hampshire* sit the longest United States place-names consisting of town/city and state—the contiguous *Hillsborough Lower Village, New Hampshire,* and *Hillsborough Upper Village, New Hampshire*—both thirty-six letters. *Charleston* (South Carolina, West Virginia, etc.) is the longest (ten letters) isogram among well-known cities. That is, it contains no repeated letters.

★ *New Mexico* is the longest state name consisting entirely of alternating consonants and vowels (within each word). *Alabama, Arizona, Colorado, Delaware, Oregon, Nevada, Texas,* and *Utah* also adhere to this pattern.

★ *New York* is the only state whose capital ends in the initials of the state itself—*Albany.*

★ It's a foregone conclusion that if you lop off the first and last letters of *foregone* you end up with *Oregon.*

★ *South Dakota* is the only state that shares no letters with its own capital—*Pierre.*

★ *Tennessee* yields the best rebus—a representation of a word composed entirely of numbers and letters—in this case, *10SE.* In addition, the possessive form, *Tennessee's,* constitutes a pyramid word—one *t,* two *n*'s, three *s*'s and four *e*'s.

★ *Florida, Vermont,* and *Wyoming* are the longest stately isograms—words with no letters repeated. *New York* is the longest two-word isogram among the states.

One last stately fact: When the names of the forty-eight contiguous states are alphabetized, half start with *A–M* and half with *N–Z.* In addition, exactly one-third (sixteen) start with *A–L,* one third with *M–N,* and one-third with *O–Z.* The *M–N* cluster divides perfectly between eight states beginning with *M* and eight beginning with *N.* ★

CHAPTER 24

PRIDE OF PLACE

WE ARE ONE of the world's most urban populations, with 83 percent of us living in cities or suburbs, as compared with a worldwide average of 50.5 percent. Since 1990, the number of Americans living

in cities has gone up 7 percent. Our ten most populous American cities are 1. New York, 2. Los Angeles, 3. Chicago, 4. Houston, 5. Philadelphia, 6. Phoenix, 7. San Antonio, 8. Dallas, 9. San Diego, and 10. San Jose. Here are some fascinating facts about our metropolitan clusters, as well as our towns:

★ **RUGBY**, **NORTH DAKOTA**, is the geographical center of North America.

★ The oldest continuously inhabited village is **ORAIBI**, **ARIZONA**, a Hopi Indian settlement established before AD 1100. It's at least five hundred years older than New York City.

★ Founded in 1565 by Spanish explorers, **ST. AUGUSTINE**, **FLORIDA**, is the oldest continuously inhabited, European-established city and port in the continental United States.

★ **PHILADELPHIA** is the home of Independence National Historical Park, "America's Most Historic Square Mile." Among its many landmarks are

"IT HAS ALWAYS BEEN CITED AS AN IRREPRESSIBLE SYMPTOM OF AMERICA'S VITALITY THAT HER PEOPLE, IN FAIR TIMES AND FOUL, BELIEVE IN THEMSELVES AND THEIR INSTITUTIONS."—*Alistair Cooke*

Independence Hall, Carpenters' Hall, Christ Church, and the Liberty Bell.

★ **KANSAS CITY** calls itself "Paris on the Plains" and "The City of Fountains" because it claims to have more miles of boulevards than Paris and more fountains than any other city save Rome.

★ According to American lore, Peter Minuit bought the island of **MANHATTAN** from its Native American inhabitants for twenty-four dollars worth of trinkets. Today the population of New York City is around 8,400,000, exceeding that of dozens of countries. That figure accounts for about 43 percent of New York State's population. New York City is not only densely populated (26,403 people per square mile), it is also ethnically rich. New York City is home to the largest number of Italians outside Italy, the largest number of Irish outside Ireland, the largest number of Jews outside Israel, and the largest number of Puerto Ricans outside Puerto Rico.

★ The full name of **LOS ANGELES** is El Pueblo de Nuestra Señora la Reina de Los Angeles de Porciúncula. It can be abbreviated to 3.63 percent of its size: L.A.

★ **LEADVILLE, COLORADO**, at 10,152 feet above sea level, is the highest city in the United States. It's the only city in Lake County. Its airport, at 9,927 feet, is the highest in the United States and its golf course, Mount Massive, is the highest in the United States at 9,680 feet. Leadville is named for the lead that was mined there. It also had rich deposits of gold, silver, zinc, and copper. In the late nineteenth century, when the mines were all working, it was the second largest city in Colorado after Denver, but the population has declined ever since and now stands at 2,682. The main industry now is tourism.

★ **ALMA, COLORADO**, an unincorporated town near Leadville, is, at 10,578 feet elevation, the highest town with permanent residents in the United States.

★ **SYRACUSE, NEW YORK**, is our snowiest city, accumulating an annual average of 118.8 inches of the fluffy stuff. **HILO, HAWAII**, receives the most rain (annual average: 126.27 inches). **JUNEAU, ALASKA**, is visited least by the sun (30 percent of the time), while **YUMA, ARIZONA**, bakes in the most sun (90 percent of the time). There's a rumor that Arizona farmers feed their hens crushed ice so that they won't lay hard-boiled eggs.

★ Four state capitals commemorate four presidents—**JEFFERSON CITY, MISSOURI; MADISON, WISCONSIN; JACKSON, MISSISSIPPI;** and **LINCOLN, NEBRASKA.**

★ The capital city of **TEXAS** was changed fifteen times (hey, it's a ginormous state!) before the citizenry finally settled on **AUSTIN.** Alaskans wanted to change their capital from Juneau to Anchorage but were put off by the cost, apparently not a problem for Texans.

★ **BOSTON, MASSACHUSETTS**, has served the longest continuous tenure as a colony/state capital, since 1630. Santa Fe, New Mexico, has actually been a capital longer, since 1610, but its tenure was interrupted by the Pueblo Rebellion from 1680 to 1692.

★ **PORTLAND, OREGON**, could very well have been called Boston. The city was founded by two New Englanders, one from Maine, the other from Massachusetts. They decided to flip a coin to see who would name the new town: heads, Portland; tails, Boston. The Maine man won the flip.

★ **ATLANTIC CITY** inspired the board game Monopoly. The city boasts the world's longest boardwalk, extending almost six miles. Built in 1870, the boardwalk's initial purpose was to keep visitors from tracking sand into hotel lobbies.

★ From **DETROIT**, in what direction would you travel to reach Canada? The answer is south. Detroit is the only major U. S. city that sits north of Canadian territory.

★ In one way, Maine is our most "cosmopolitan" state, because within its borders sit towns named **CHINA, DENMARK, EGYPT, MEXICO, NORWAY, PERU, POLAND,** and **SWEDEN.**

City Nicknames

Identify the cities that have inspired these notable nicknames:

1. The Big Apple ★ 2. The Windy City ★ 3. Beantown ★ 4. The City of Brotherly Love ★ 5. The Big Easy ★ 6. The Mile-High City ★ 7. The Heart of Bluegrass Country ★ 8. Motown ★ 9. The Entertainment Capital of the World ★ 10. Big D ★ 11. Music City ★ 12. The Golden Gate City

Answers

1. New York ★ 2. Chicago ★ 3. Boston ★ 4. Philadelphia ★ 5. New Orleans ★ 6. Denver ★ 7. Lexington ★ 8. Detroit ★ 9. Los Angeles ★ 10. Dallas ★ 11. Nashville ★ 12. San Francisco

CHAPTER 25

AMERICA GROWS UP

THE ESTIMATED EUROPEAN POPULATION in 1610 of the land that was to become the United States of America was 350 souls. By the time the first official census of the thirteen United States was taken, in 1790, we had grown by more than ten-thousand-fold to 3,929,214 residents.

Article 1, section 2 of the Constitution of the United States mandates that an "actual Enumeration" of the nation's population be made every ten years so that "representatives and direct Taxes shall be apportioned among the several States which may be included within this Union, according to their respective Numbers." Here's a decade-by-decade look at the growth of the American people since then:

1800 — 5,308,483	*1860* — 31,443,321	*1920* — 106,021,537	*1980* — 226,545,805
1810 — 7,239,881	*1870* — 38,558,371	*1930* — 123,202,624	*1990* — 248,709,873
1820 — 9,638,453	*1880* — 50,189,209	*1940* — 132,164,569	*2000* — 281,421,906
1830 — 12,866,020	*1890* — 62,979,766	*1950* — 151,325,798	*2010* — 308,745,538
1840 — 17,069,453	*1900* — 76,212,168	*1960* — 179,323,175	
1850 — 23,191,876	*1910* — 92,228,496	*1970* — 203,211,926	

★ ★ ★ ★

PART 6

Ties That Bind

★ ★ ★ ★

CHAPTER 26

FOOD FOR THOUGHT

ONE OF THE THREADS that weaves us together into families, communities, and a nation is food. We gather in homes, restaurants, fellowship halls, parks, sports stadiums, and at the beach for potlucks, picnics, group dinners, and quiet family meals. Almost every family occasion and form of entertainment includes food as a component.

Each region boasts specialties, but some foods are found nationwide. It's hard to imagine a town, a village, or a hamlet in America where you couldn't get a hamburger and french fries. And what do you drink? A soft drink. You may call it pop, soda, tonic, or Coke, depending on where you live, but it's everywhere. Americans consume more than fifty gallons of the sweet, fizzy stuff per person per year.

Soda has a long history in America. In 1806, Benjamin Silliman sold the first artificial mineral water in New Haven, Connecticut. The first soda fountains were manufactured in the 1830s. And in 1899, the first Coca-Cola bottling plant opened in Atlanta, Georgia.

Some sodas are available nationwide; others are regional favorites. The brands and varieties seem endless. One Internet vendor offers sixty-six root beer brands, sixty-four cream sodas, forty-two ginger ales and ginger beers, thirty-nine colas, sixteen birch beers, eleven sarsaparillas, and ten chocolates.

You're probably familiar with orange, grape, and lemon-lime. Maybe you've tried black cherry or grapefruit. But what about pineapple, green apple, or peach? Not wild enough? How about honeydew, watermelon, huckleberry, marionberry, or kumquat? Still too tame? Then there's celery, cucumber, lavender, ginseng, rhubarb, and juniper berry. There are even sodas that mimic the harder stuff—mojito, Chianti, amaretto, lime rickey, and julep.

The original **COCA-COLA** contained cocaine, which came from one of its ingredients, coca leaves. All the cocaine was removed after 1905. The caffeine, which came from cola nuts, remained. Coca-Cola went on to become the world's most popular soft drink.

PEPSI-COLA was named Brad's Drink when Caleb Bradham created it in 1893. He was trying to concoct a fountain drink that would aid digestion. He changed the name to Pepsi-Cola in 1898.

Created in 1929, **7UP** was originally called Bib-Label Lithiated Lemon-Lime Soda. It's easy to see why that mouthful was condensed.

★ We Americans are definitely sweet in the tooth. In addition to gulping down vats of soda, we ingest tons of **CANDY.** In 2009, the per capita candy consumption in the United States was 24.3 lbs. Did you receive your share of Valentine Conversation Hearts, Peeps, chocolate Easter eggs, candy kisses, and candy corn?

★ **ICE CREAM** was invented in Europe in the 1600s, but after it reached the American colonies around 1700 the confection has become known as the "Great American Dessert." The earliest known ad for the treat appeared in the 1770s, and the first ice cream shop opened in New York City in 1776. In 1790, George Washington paid $200, a hefty sum in those days, for ice cream

equipment and recipes. Two presidents later, Thomas Jefferson had his special recipe for vanilla ice cream and, in 1802, became the first to serve ice cream in the White House.

★ The **ICE CREAM CONE** made its American debut at the 1904 St. Louis World's Fair, which celebrated the centennial of the Louisiana Purchase. One of a number of stories about the invention of the ice cream cone is that a Syrian immigrant named Ernest Hamwi gave some of his zalabia, a waffle-like food, to a neighboring vendor who had run out of paper plates to hold the ice cream.

★ Somebody once defined a **HAMBURGER** as "a humble immigrant hunk of meat that came to this country and soared to fame on a bun." That somebody was right. The hamburger, named after a city in Germany, began life in Europe as *Hamburg steak,* ultimately shortened to *hamburger.* In 1891 in Tulsa, Oklahoma, the patty first snuggled into a bun.

The first McDonald's was a San Bernardino, California, drive-in opened in 1940 by two brothers, Richard and Maurice McDonald. They prepared and sold a large volume of hamburgers, french fries, and milk shakes with assembly-line production. **RAY KROC** (1902–1984) sold milk-shake mixers to the brothers. Kroc partnered with the brothers in 1954 to help with franchising, eventually buying them out in 1961 for one million dollars each, after taxes. Commenting that a hamburger restaurant named Kroc's wouldn't attract many customers, Kroc opened his first new McDonald's in 1955 in Des Plains, Illinois. Then he began selling franchises for new restaurants. One of his many innovations was the training program he instituted for owner-managers—Hamburger University in Oak Brook, Illinois. Today McDonald's is one of the world's largest food-service retailers.

★ **SPAM**, an acronym for spiced ham, is manufactured in Austin, Minnesota, and Fremont, Nebraska. The product was introduced in 1937. The seven billionth can was sold in 2007, and 3.8 cans of the stuff are consumed every second in the United States. It's so popular on Pacific islands that Guam, Hawaii, and Saipan have McDonald's restaurants that feature SPAM.

★ **POTATOES** were first planted in New Hampshire in 1719. At a White House dinner in 1802, Thomas Jefferson presented "potatoes served in the French manner." By the early twentieth

"THE BUSINESS OF AMERICA IS BUSINESS."
—*Calvin Coolidge*

century, "french fried" came to mean "deep fried." Nowadays, 22 percent of the American potato crop is french fried.

★ In 1787, Jefferson introduced **PASTA** to the United States. When he served as ambassador to France, he grew to love the taste of pasta so much that he ordered a pasta-making machine sent back to the United States—the first "macaroni maker" in America. Quite the gourmet, Jefferson is also credited with introducing anchovies, olive oil, and Parmesan cheese to the States.

★ Americans spend more than $6.4 billion a year on **READY-TO-EAT CEREAL**. The Cheerios brand accounts for one in every eight boxes sold in the United States. General Mills debuted CheeriOats in 1941 and changed the

name to Cheerios four years later. The little *o*'s are made with "puffing gun" technology, in which balls of dough are heated and shot out of a gun at hundreds of miles an hour to create the iconic round shape.

★ **LOBSTERS** were so plentiful in colonial New England that they were considered food fit for only the poorest Americans, those who could not afford anything better. (We, your faithful authors, wonder, when a restaurant serves you "twin lobsters," how they can know that for sure?)

★ The United States is one of the largest producers of **APPLES** in the world. The Roxbury Russet apple is probably the first named American apple. It has been grown here since the mid-1600s and is good for eating and for making juice and cider.

★ Far from being a whimsical ne'er-do-well as portrayed in movies and popular literature, **JOHN CHAPMAN** (1774–1845), also known as **JOHNNY APPLESEED,** was a trained nurseryman and a canny businessman who started a series of plant nurseries on the frontier and had a needed product waiting when settlers arrived. That product was apple seedlings.

Johnny Appleseed was responsible for planting more than a hundred thousand acres of apple orchards.

Apples don't grow true from seed. That means if you have a wonderful apple tree and you plant the seeds, you won't get another wonderful apple tree. You'll probably get apples that are just about inedible. That didn't matter to Johnny or to his customers.

They weren't buying eating apples; they were buying apple trees for cider making. Hard cider was the usual drink at a time when water was unsafe.

Johnny planted apple trees and left them in the care of a local resident. Once a year or so, he dropped by to tend the trees and divide profits with his local representative. In 1800, he started selling apple seedlings to settlers in Pennsylvania, Ohio, Indiana, Illinois, and Kentucky. Over the course of his lifetime, Johnny Appleseed was responsible for the planting of more than a hundred thousand acres of apple orchards across our land.

★ **CRACKER JACK** was developed for the World's Columbian Exposition in Chicago in 1893. According to the Cracker Jack website, if all the Cracker Jack ever sold were laid end to end, it would circle the Earth more than sixty-nine times. They don't tell us whether this is boxes or individual pieces, but in either case, it's a lot. They have given out more than 23 billion toys since

> **"AMERICA HAS BELIEVED THAT IN DIFFERENTIATION, NOT IN UNIFORMITY, LIES THE PATH OF PROGRESS. IT ACTED ON THIS BELIEF; IT HAS ADVANCED HUMAN HAPPINESS, AND IT HAS PROSPERED."**—*Louis Brandeis*

they first started including them in the boxes in 1912, almost thirty years after Cracker Jack first appeared. By the way, the boy on the Cracker Jack box is Jack; his dog's name is Bingo.

★ **CHILI PEPPERS** were introduced into the American diet and to the rest of the world from Native Americans in the Southwest. In 1912, American pharmacist Wilbur Scoville devised the Scoville Organoleptic Test, a scale for measuring the hotness of chili peppers. The scale ranges from 0 SHU (Scoville heat units) for a sweet bell pepper, through 5,500 SHU for a Jalapeno, to 1,000,000+ SHU for a bih/bhut jolokia.

★ **BARNUM'S ANIMALS**, more popularly known as animal crackers, came in a box that looked like a circus wagon and with a string attached because the small package was originally hung on Christmas trees.

★ **FORTUNE COOKIES** are entirely an American invention, created for Chinese restaurants in America. You will not find them in establishments in China. Here are some typical messages found inside fortune cookies: "You are guided by silent love and friendship around you." "Patience is the best remedy for every trouble." "Appearances can be deceiving." What do these statements have in common? They're not fortunes; they're words of wisdom or statements about character. Have a look at the strips of paper you release from your next fortune cookies, and you'll find that more than half of them don't tell your fortune. ★

CHAPTER 27

WE ALL SPEAK MOVIE LINES

AMERICANS HAVE FALLEN deeply in love with that beguiling conspiracy of light and darkness and color and silence and sound and music that we call the movies. The late director Sidney Lumet said, "Nothing can tell you more about America than the movies."

THE GREAT TRAIN ROBBERY, an eleven-minute, silent, black-and-white film produced in 1903, was the first to tell an extended story. It was also the first commercially successful film, earning $150, big bucks back then. This "western" was actually shot in New Jersey, our nation's film capital until the more benign weather of Los Angeles lured away the filmmakers.

In 1927, Warner Brothers released ***THE JAZZ SINGER,*** the first feature-length film with synchronized speech and sound effects. Its star was **AL JOLSON** (1886–1950). Jolson sang six songs in the movie, but there were only two minutes of spoken dialogue. That was enough. The audience was electrified by what it heard. Silent movies were on the way out.

In the movie theater—and increasingly on smaller screens—the boundaries between real and reel, the line between reality and movies, wavers and blurs. Something has happened to our American language—and we've a feeling we're not in Kansas anymore.

You'll probably recognize the second part of that statement as a borrowing from the film **THE WIZARD OF OZ.** Being transported out of Kansas is one of a passel of expressions from movies that have launched a thousand lips.

The very first Academy Awards ceremony took place during a banquet held in the Blossom Room of the Hollywood Roosevelt Hotel. Two hundred seventy people attended and tickets cost $10. When the first awards were handed out on May 16, 1929, movies had just begun to talk. We would love to have been a time traveler rushing into the Blossom Room to announce the luminous future of the Academy Awards ceremony:

"Wait a minute! Wait a minute! You ain't heard nothing yet!" That's what Al Jolson said in **THE JAZZ SINGER.** Ever since, lines from the movies have shaped our hopes and dreams and aspirations, and have suffused our everyday conversations.

Today we're making you an offer you can't refuse—a version of the line in Mario Puzo's novel, **THE GODFATHER,** published in 1969, and embedded in the 1972 film of the same name.

So what's up, Doc? That is, of course, from Bugs Bunny's characteristic question to Elmer Fudd. What's up is that we hope never to hear from our readers, "What we have here is a failure to communicate" or "I'm mad as hell, and I'm not going to take it anymore!"

The first statement began as a line in **COOL HAND LUKE,** and the second is Peter Finch's furious complaint in **NETWORK.**

May you never sneer at us, "Frankly, my dear, I don't give a damn," spoken by Clark Gable in **GONE WITH THE WIND.** But that's okay, because tomorrow is another day.

Indeed, we think this is the beginning of a beautiful friendship, a line delivered by Humphrey Bogart in **CASABLANCA.** That film also gave us "Round up the usual suspects" and "Here's looking at you, kid."

Plunge ahead, gentle reader, and you'll go ahead, make my day—the signature statement of the Clint Eastwood character Dirty Harry in the 1983 film **SUDDEN IMPACT,** a line made even more famous by President Ronald Reagan.

You'll make our day because love is never having to say you're sorry, an enduring sentiment from **LOVE STORY.**

Who you gonna call?—your faithful *American Trivia* authors! That's a spin-off from **GHOSTBUSTERS,** and, of course, it should be "whom are you going to call?"

Now identify the films whence came the following expressions that inhabit our everyday conversations:

1. They're ba-a-a-ck!
2. If you build it, he will come.
3. Houston, we have a problem.
4. Life is like a box of chocolates.
5. You talkin' to me?
6. I coulda been a contender!
7. Why don't you come up sometime and see me?
8. The end of civilization as we now know it.
9. May the Force be with you!
10. Show me the money!

Answers

1. *Poltergeist* ★ 2. *Field of Dreams* ★ 3. *Apollo 13* ★ 4. *Forrest Gump* ★ 5. *Taxi Driver* ★ 6. *On the Waterfront* ★ 7. *She Done Him Wrong* ★ 8. *Citizen Kane* ★ 9. *Star Wars* ★ 10. *Jerry Maguire*

That's all, folks! *Hasta la vista,* baby!—and you know where those two lines got their start: Merry Melodies and **TERMINATOR 2: JUDGMENT DAY** ★

CHAPTER 28

A BASEBALL DOUBLE-HEADER

AMERICA IS A SPORTS-LOVING NATION. Throughout their lives, Americans invest considerable money, time, and passion in playing sports and following the exploits of teams and individual athletes. Most schools and colleges are represented by a coterie of sports teams, and the morale of a major city rises and falls with the successes and stumbles of its school and professional teams.

The four most popular team sports in this country—baseball, football, basketball, and ice hockey—all began life in North America. We can't begin to cover all sports within the brief compass of this book, so we're focusing on baseball, which has justly been called the "national pastime."

Baseball is one of our oldest sports, originating before the Civil War as a game called rounders. Abraham Lincoln played town ball, a local variant of rounders, and may have been playing that game when, in 1860, the news reached him that he had been elected president.

Our chief executives have been tossing out the opening-day baseball since April 14, 1910, when William Howard Taft started the tradition, attending a game between Clark Griffith's Washington Senators and Connie Mack's Philadelphia Athletics. Taft was not expecting to be asked to make that first pitch. Nonetheless, he executed a creditable throw, if a little low.

"AMERICA IS STILL THE BEST COUNTRY FOR THE COMMON MAN— WHITE OR BLACK . . . IF HE CAN'T MAKE IT HERE, HE WON'T MAKE IT ANYWHERE ELSE."
—*Eric Hoffer*

On June 19, 1846, in a contest many historians consider the first scheduled baseball game, the New York Baseball Club defeated the Knickerbocker Baseball Club 23–1 in four innings. With more than a century and a half of American history, baseball evokes more nostalgia than any other athletic endeavor. No other sports poem is as beloved as Ernest Lawrence Thayer's "Casey at the Bat," published in 1888; and no other sports song is nearly as famous as "Take Me Out to the Ball Game," first recorded in 1908.

More fans than in any other sport know the key statistics of baseball— most hits (**PETE ROSE**, 4,256), most wins (**CY YOUNG**, 511), most strikeouts (**NOLAN RYAN**, 5,714), most home runs in a season and over a career (**BARRY BONDS**, 73, 762), most stolen bases (**RICKEY HENDERSON**, 1,406), most consecutive games played (**CAL RIPKEN JR.**, 2,632), and on and on.

To help you pass time, here are two games—a veritable doubleheader— about our national pastime:

A Baseball Game

TY COBB's lifetime batting average is .366, eight points higher than that of anyone else. He won eleven batting titles, batting .401 at the age of thirty-five and .323 at the age of forty-one.

Long after his retirement, a newspaper reporter asked Cobb how he would do playing modern baseball. "I figure I'd bat around .280," Cobb replied.

"Only .280?" asked the reporter. "But your lifetime batting average was .366." "Yep," replied Cobb. "But keep in mind that I'm fifty-four years old."

From the descriptions below, identify each baseball star. Answers slide in at the end of the game.

1. Inducted in 1936, the first five members of the Baseball Hall of Fame were **TY COBB**, **BABE RUTH**, **HONUS WAGNER**, **CHRISTY MATHEWSON**, and _____, a pitcher nicknamed the "Big Train," who won 417 games, second only to Cy Young.

2. First a pitcher, then an outfielder, _____ broke the single-season home run record four times and led the New York Yankees to seven World Series championships.

3. The son of Italian immigrants, _____ achieved the American dream: Born in a small town, Martinez, California, he grew up to star for the New York Yankees. From May 15 to July 16, 1941, the Yankee Clipper hit safely in fifty-six straight games, a record that has stood for more than seventy years. He married the most glamorous movie star of his day. And he is immortalized in Simon and Garfunkel's song "Mrs. Robinson."

4. In 1947, a courageous _____ broke the color barrier in baseball, becoming the first African American to play in the major leagues. Over the course of a decade, he led the Brooklyn Dodgers to six World Series and one World Series Championship.

5. Cy Young winner _____ skipped the first game of the 1965 World Series in Bloomington, Minnesota, because it fell on Yom

Kippur. Willie Stargell said that trying to hit this pitcher "was like trying to drink coffee with a fork."

6. In 1948, _____ became the oldest rookie in baseball when he signed with the Cleveland Indians on what was believed to have been his forty-second birthday. Before that he had starred as a pitcher in the Negro Leagues. In 1965, he threw three shutout innings for the Kansas City Athletics in his last trip to the mound.

7. Splendid Splinter _____ was the last baseball player to end a season with a batting average over .400 (.406 in 1941). He twice sacrificed his career to serve his country,

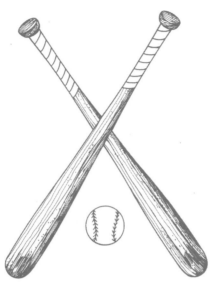

first in World War II and then in Korea.

8. Even though _____ never hit more than forty-seven home runs in a single season, his career total of 755 home runs broke Babe Ruth's record and stood for thirty-three years. He still owns the record for the most career runs batted in, 2,297.

Answers

1. Walter Johnson ★ 2. Babe Ruth ★ 3. Joe DiMaggio ★ 4 Jackie Robinson ★ 5. Sandy Koufax ★ 6. Leroy "Satchel" Paige ★ 7. Ted Williams ★ 8. Hank Aaron

Play Ball!

Because sports occupy such a central place in American life and imagination, athletic metaphors pervade our speech and writing. There's a democratic poetry in the sporty phrases that color our everyday vocabulary, and these expressions are

vivid emblems of the games that we, as an American people, watch and play.

In the early days of the twentieth century, a college professor explained, "To understand America, you must understand baseball." Not only is baseball America's pastime, but the source of the most pervasive athletic metaphors in the American language. Whether or not we're fans, we speak baseballese just about every day of our lives.

Fill in each blank below with a common word or phrase that has its origins in baseball. Don't worry. We won't throw you any curveballs. In fact, right off the bat, we'll throw you a fat one right down the middle: "We know you won't quit. You'll always be *in there pitching*."

Answers cross the plate at the end of this game.

1. We're not making a bit of progress with this project. We can't even get to _____ _____.

2. You are so out of it. You're way out there in _____ _____.

3. Some people are born with a silver spoon in their mouth, while others are born with _____ _____ against them.

4. Everybody's so enthusiastic about your proposal. You just hit a _____ _____.

5. I know you can't give me an exact price, but can you give me a _____ figure?

6. These people are really serious. They play _____.

7. On Broadway, the new musical comedy has been a _____ _____.

8. I promise I'll consult you before I make any decisions. I'll be sure to _____ _____ with you.

9. I can't meet with you today, but I'd like to in the near future. May I take a _____ _____?

10. Before we submit the proposal, we need to _____ _____ a few ideas.

11. She's such a wild and wacky woman—a real _____.

12. Throckmorton is away at a conference, so we're going to have Gump _____ _____ for him.

13. That business presentation was great. It was a _____ _____ performance.

14. They're inexperienced, and they're incompetent. They run a _____ _____ operation.

15. Greg will stay single for the rest of his life. Rather than settling down, he prefers to _____ _____ _____.

Answers

1. first base ★ 2. left field ★ 3. two strikes ★ 4. home run ★ 5. ballpark ★ 6. hardball ★ 7. smash hit ★ 8. touch base ★ 9. rain check ★ 10. bat around ★ 11. screwball ★ 12. pinch-hit ★ 13. major league ★ 14. bush league/ minor league ★ 15. play the field

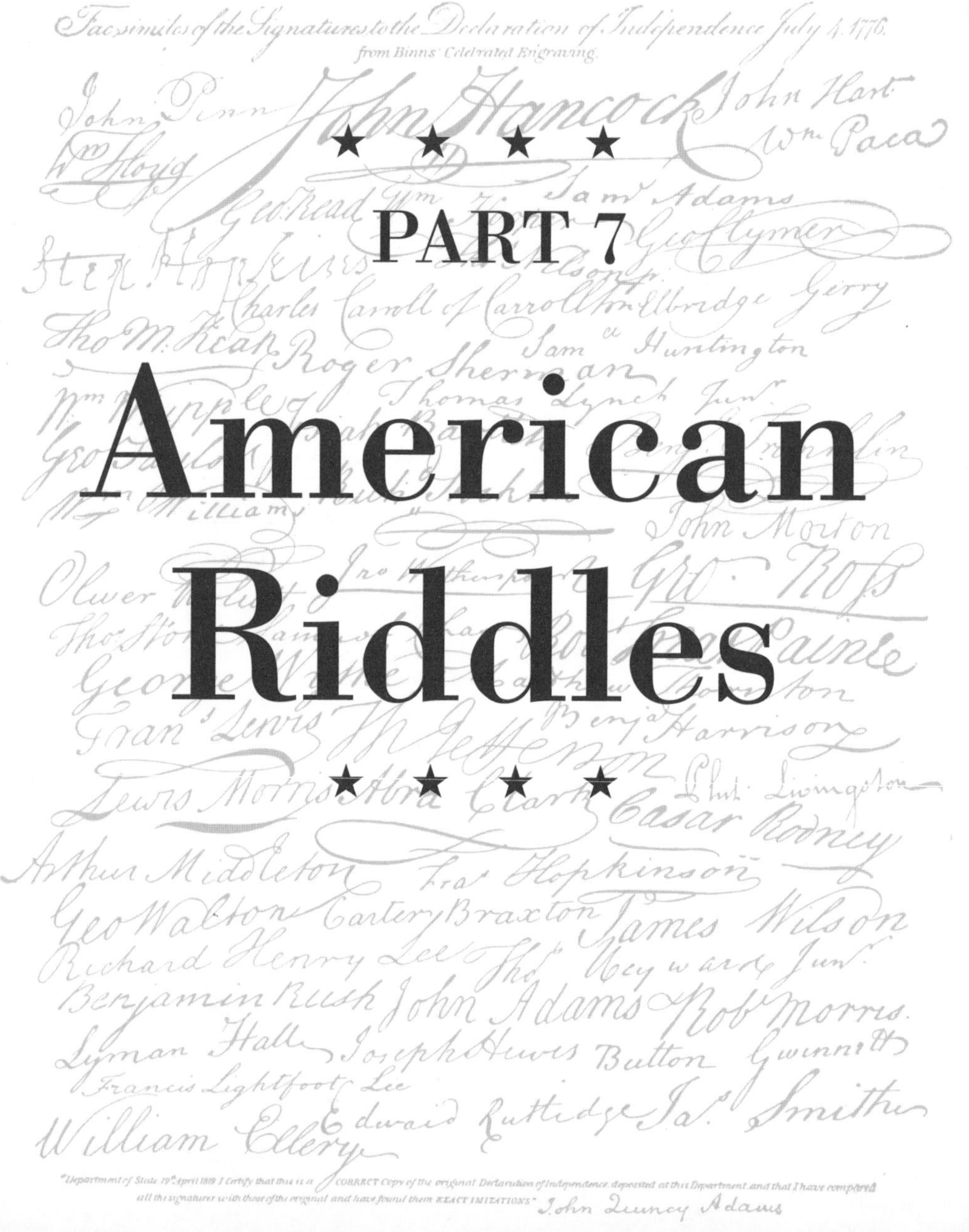

★ ★ ★ ★

PART 7

American Riddles

★ ★ ★ ★

The National Assessment of Educational Progress tests what American students are learning and not learning and acts as "the nation's report card." Results of the NAEP examinations show that the two worst subjects for American students are civics and American history. For example, one NAEP survey found that only 7 percent of eighth graders can describe the three branches of government. In other polls, one-quarter of high school students said that Columbus set sail after 1750, and one-third couldn't identify the century in which the Revolutionary War was fought.

Perhaps the riddles that follow may boost your knowledge and demonstrate that learning the history of our country can be a lot of fun.

HOW DO WE KNOW THAT COLUMBUS WAS THE BEST DEALMAKER IN HISTORY?
He left not knowing where he was going. When he got there, he didn't know where he was. When he returned, he didn't know where he'd been. And he did it all on borrowed money.

HOW DID KING FERDINAND AND QUEEN ISABELLA PAY FOR COLUMBUS'S VOYAGES?
With their Discover card.

WHAT DO THE *NIÑA*, THE *PINTA*, AND THE *SANTA MARIA* HAVE IN COMMON WITH A DEPARTMENT STORE?
They're all driven by sails.

HOW DO WE KNOW THAT COLUMBUS'S SHIPS GOT THE BEST GAS MILEAGE IN HISTORY?
  They got three thousand miles per galleon.

WHAT IS THE FRUITIEST SUBJECT IN SCHOOL?
  History. It's full of dates.

IF APRIL SHOWERS BRING MAY FLOWERS, WHAT DO MAY FLOWERS BRING?
  Pilgrims.

WHAT WAS THE PILGRIMS' FAVORITE KIND OF MUSIC?
  Plymouth Rock.

WHY DID THE PILGRIMS' PANTS
ALWAYS FALL DOWN?
  Because they wore their buckles on
  their hats.

WHY WERE THE EARLY AMERICAN
SETTLERS LIKE ANTS?
  Because they lived in colonies.

WHICH COLONISTS MADE THE
MOST WRITING INSTRUMENTS?
  Pen-sylvanians (or Pencil-vanians).

WHICH COLONISTS TOLD
THE MOST JOKES?
  Pun-sylvanians.

WHAT HAPPENED AS A RESULT
OF THE STAMP ACT?
  The Americans licked the British.

WHAT KIND OF TEA DID THE
AMERICAN COLONISTS
THIRST FOR?
  Liber-Tea.

WHAT DID KING GEORGE THINK
OF THE AMERICAN COLONISTS?
  He found them revolting.

WHAT DID THE COLONISTS WEAR
AT THE BOSTON TEA PARTY?
  Tea-shirts.

WHAT PROTEST BY A GROUP
OF DOGS OCCURRED IN 1773?
  The Boston Flea Party.

WHY DID PAUL REVERE RIDE
HIS HORSE FROM BOSTON
TO LEXINGTON?
  Because the horse was too heavy to
  carry.

WHAT DANCE WAS VERY POPULAR
IN 1776?
  Indepen-dance.

WHAT DID ONE FLAG SAY
TO THE OTHER FLAG?
  Nothing. It just waved.

DID YOU HEAR THE JOKE ABOUT
THE LIBERTY BELL?
  Yeah, it cracked me up.

WHAT'S BIG, CRACKED, AND
CARRIES YOUR LUGGAGE?
  The Liberty Bell-hop.

WHERE WAS THE DECLARATION
OF INDEPENDENCE SIGNED?
  At the bottom.

WHAT'S RED, WHITE, BLACK,
AND BLUE?
  Uncle Sam falling down the steps.

WHAT HAS FOUR LEGS, A SHINY
NOSE, AND FOUGHT FOR ENGLAND?
  Rudolph the Redcoat Reindeer.

WHAT DID THE COLONISTS
CALL THE BARNYARD FOWL
THEY TRAINED TO CAPTURE
BRITISH SPIES?
  Chicken catch-a-Tory.

WHAT WOULD YOU GET IF YOU CROSSED GEORGE WASHINGTON'S HOME WITH NASTY INSECTS?
MOUNT VERMIN.

WHAT WOULD YOU GET IF YOU CROSSED GEORGE WASHINGTON WITH CATTLE FEED?

The Fodder of Our Country.

WHAT WOULD YOU GET IF YOU CROSSED OUR FIRST PRESIDENT WITH A WOOD SCULPTOR?

George Washington Carver.

WHAT IS THE DIFFERENCE BETWEEN A DUCK AND GEORGE WASHINGTON.

The duck has a bill on its face and Washington has his face on a bill.

WHICH ONE OF GEORGE WASHINGTON'S OFFICERS HAD THE BEST SENSE OF HUMOR?

Laugh-ayette.

IF GEORGE WASHINGTON WERE ALIVE TODAY, WHY COULDN'T HE THROW A SILVER DOLLAR ACROSS THE POTOMAC?

Because a dollar doesn't go as far as it used to.

WHAT WOULD YOU GET IF YOU CROSSED A PATRIOT WITH A SMALL, CURLY-HAIRED DOG?

A Yankee Poodle.

DID YOU HEAR ABOUT THE TALENTED CARTOONIST IN THE CONTINENTAL ARMY?

He was a dandy Yankee doodler.

WHAT WAS GENERAL WASHINGTON'S FAVORITE TREE?

The infan-tree.

WHAT DID WASHINGTON SAY AS HE STOOD ON THE BOAT CROSSING THE DELAWARE?
"Next time I'm going to reserve a seat."

IF GEORGE WASHINGTON WERE ALIVE TODAY, WHAT WOULD HE BE FAMOUS FOR?
Old age.

WHAT COUNTERFEITERS WERE ACTIVE DURING THE AMERICAN REVOLUTION?
The Valley Forgers.

WHAT DID BENJAMIN FRANKLIN'S POLITICAL OPPONENTS SAY TO HIM WHENEVER THEY GOT ANGRY AT HIM?
"Go fly a kite!"

WHAT HAS FEATHERS, WEBBED FEET, AND CERTAIN UNALIENABLE RIGHTS?
The Duck-laration of Independence.

WHERE DID GEORGE WASHINGTON BUY HIS HATCHET?
At the chopping mall.

HOW IS A HEALTHY PERSON LIKE THE UNITED STATES?
They both have good constitutions.

WHY DID THE DUCK SAY "BANG!" ON THE FOURTH OF JULY?

Because he was a fire-quacker.

WHAT DID BETSY ROSS DO WHEN SHE ASKED SOME COLONISTS THEIR OPINION OF THE FLAG SHE HAD MADE?

She invented the first flag poll.

WHAT WAS THOMAS JEFFERSON'S FAVORITE MUSICAL INSTRUMENT?

The Monti-cello.

WHAT WOULD YOU GET IF YOU CROSSED THE AMERICAN NATIONAL BIRD WITH SNOOPY?

A bald beagle.

WHO INVENTED THE GRANDFATHER CLOCK?

Pendulum Franklin.

HOW MANY EARS DID DAVY CROCKETT HAVE?

Three—his left ear, his right ear, and his wild front ear.

WHY DO AMERICANS LIKE TO WEAR SHORT-SLEEVED SHIRTS?

It reminds them of their right to bare arms.

WHY DO AMERICANS GIVE GUNS TO GRIZZLIES?

Because we have the right to arm bears.

★ AMERICAN RIDDLES ★

WHICH AMERICAN PRESIDENT
IS THE LEAST GUILTY?
Abraham Lincoln. He's in a cent.

WHAT'S THE DIFFERENCE BETWEEN
CUSTARD AND CUSTER?
One is full of sugar. The other is full of arrows.

HOW CAN WE TELL THAT
THE STATUE OF LIBERTY
LOVES AMERICA?
She carries a torch for us.

WHO WAS ALEXANDER GRAHAM
BELLOFSKY?
The first telephone Pole.

WHY WAS THOMAS EDISON
EXHAUSTED AFTER HE INVENTED
THE LIGHT BULB?
Because he wasn't able to sleep with the light on.

WHAT KIND OF ELECTRICITY DO
THEY HAVE IN WASHINGTON?
D.C.

WHAT'S RED, WHITE, BLUE,
AND GREEN?
A patriotic pickle.

WHAT DID PEOPLE CALL FDR
AND HIS MORAY, WHICH NEVER
WORE ANY CLOTHING?
Franklin Roosevelt and the Nude Eel.

HOW DO WE KNOW THAT ANYONE
CAN BECOME PRESIDENT OF
THE UNITED STATES?
Jefferson did it. Nixon did it. And Truman did it. So any Tom, Dick, and Harry can be president.